'BAPTISED IN BLOOD'

*The Formation
of
The Cork Brigade of Irish Volunteers
1913–1916*

GERRY WHITE AND BRENDAN O'SHEA

Published in association with

Cork Public Museum

ꟽERCIER PRESS

MERCIER PRESS
Douglas Village, Cork
www.mercierpress.ie

Trade enquiries to COLUMBA MERCIER DISTRIBUTION,
55a Spruce Avenue, Stillorgan Industrial Park, Blackrock, Dublin

© Gerry White and Brendan O'Shea 2005

1 85635 465 2

10 9 8 7 6 5 4 3 2 1

This book is dedicated to the memory of all those who established and served within the ranks of the Cork Brigade of Irish Volunteers during its formative years.

 Mercier Press receives financial assistance from
the Arts Council/An Chomhairle Ealaíon

Printed in Ireland by ColourBooks Ltd

'BAPTISED IN BLOOD'

The Formation
of
he Cork Brigade of Irish Volunteers
1913–1916

'History, after all, is in the main the sum total of individual effort, provided, of course, that men are working in unity under the inspiration of some common cause. I did my humble best and I came into contact with so many others working likewise to make the harvest fruitful … One day men will be gathering even the slightest memories of those years.'

James J. Walsh
First Chairman
The Cork Brigade of Irish Volunteers

J. J. WALSH, RECOLLECTIONS OF A REBEL

Contents

National Colours used by the Cork Brigade of Irish Volunteers
[Courtesy of Cork Public Museum]

Acknowledgements

This project could not have been brought to fruition without invaluable assistance from several people. We must extend a special word of thanks to Stella Cherry the curator of Cork Public Museum and her assistant Dan Breen. For many years now Stella and Dan have actively supported us in our research of the Irish Volunteers and we owe them both a huge debt of gratitude. The majority of the images in this book appear courtesy of the museum and we would like to thank Dara McGrath who took many of the photographs. The other members of the Museum staff who provided assistance in their own special way were Samantha Melia, Kathleen Cunningham, Douglas Walsh and Rita O'Riordan. A number of photographs and much of the archival material quoted in this book were provided courtesy of Cork Archives Institute and we wish to acknowledge the assistance given by Brian McGee the archivist, Timmy O'Connor the assistant-archivist, Michael Higgins and Peter McDonnell. The following members of the staff at the Local Studies Department in Cork City Library were also extremely helpful during long hours of research: Kieran Burke, Stephen Leach, Lucy Stewart, Caroline Long Nolan, Jamie O'Connell, John Paul McCarthy; as were the staff at Hollyhill Library: Mary Corcoran, Deirbhile Dennehy, Richie Feely and Henry Caulfield. Paddy Cremin at the museum in Collins Barracks Cork continues to be a goldmine of information regarding the history of the city of Cork and must be thanked for sharing his thoughts with us on numerous occasions; as must Lt Comdr Ken Minehane for his advice on nautical matters, Capt Tom O'Neill, Kevin Girvan, Brother Thomas Connolly of the Allen Library, Dublin and Anne Kearney of the Irish Examiner.

We are also grateful to Fionnuala MacCurtain and Máire Ní Brugha for keeping the Volunteer flame alive; to Eoin Langford for providing access to Riobárd Langford's collection of documents; to Peg McCarthy for willingly making available the papers belonging to her father (Seán Murphy); to Breda O'Donoghue Lucci for giving us access to the Florence O'Donoghue papers; to Sarah Ruiseal for providing access to Liam Ruiseal's collection; to Tom Meaney, Noreen Meaney and Siobhan Boland for providing access to papers and photographs in relation to Cornelius Meaney; to Dick Kenny for sharing his unique memories and personal insights into the Cork Brigade of Irish Volunteers; to the staff at Military Archives for their assistance; and to the many friends and colleagues in the Defence Forces who have helped on several occasions along the way.

As always without the encouragement and support shown by Mary Feehan and the staff at Mercier Press the project would never have got off the ground in the first instance.

And finally a special word of thanks to the ever-supportive White and O'Shea families whose patience has long ago worn thin.

Gerry White, Cork City
Brendan O'Shea, Monrovia, Liberia
25 May 2005

Manifesto of Irish Volunteers.

A T a time when legislative proposals universally confessed to be of vital concern for the future of Ireland have been put forward, and are awaiting decision, a plan has been deliberately adopted by one of the great English political parties, advocated by the leaders of that party and by its numerous organs in the Press, and brought systematically to bear on English public opinion, to make the display of military force and the menace of armed violence the determining factor in the future relations between this couutry and Great Britain.

The party which has thus substituted open force for the semblance of civil government is seeking by this means not merely to decide an immediate political issue of grave concern to this Nation, but also to obtain for itself the future control of all our national affairs. It is plain to every man that the people of Ireland, if they acquiesce in this new policy by their inaction, will consent to the surrender, not only of their rights as a nation, but of their civic rights as men.

The Act of Union deprived the Irish nation of the power to direct its own course and to develop and use its own resources for its own benefit. It gave us, instead, the meagre and seldom effective right of throwing our votes into the vast and complicated movement of British politics. Since the Act of Union a long series of repressive statutes has endeavoured to deal with the incessant discontent of the Irish people by depriving them of various rights common to all who live under the British Constitution. The new policy goes further than the Act of Union, and further than all subsequent Coercion Acts taken together. It proposes to leave us the political franchise in name, and to annihilate it in fact. · If we fail to take such measures as will effectually defeat this policy, we become politically the most degraded population in Europe, and no longer worthy of the name of Nation.

Are we to rest inactive, in the hope that the course of politics in Great Britain may save us from the degradation openly threatened against us? **British politics are controlled by British interests, and are complicated by problems of great importance to the people of Great Britain. In a crisis of this kind, the duty of safeguarding our own rights is our duty first and foremost.** *They have rights who dare maintain them.* If we remain quiescent, by what title can we expect the people of Great Britain to turn aside from their own pressing concerns to defend us? Will not such an attitude of itself mark us out as a people unworthy of defence.

Such is the occasion, not altogether unfortunate, which has brought about the inception of the Irish Volunteer movement. But the Volunteers, once they have been enrolled, will form a prominent element in the national life under a National Government. The Nation will maintain its Volunteer organisation as a guarantee of the liberties which the Irish people shall have secured.

If ever in history a people could say that an opportunity was given them by God's will to make an honest and manly stand for their rights, that opportunity is given us to-day.

The stress of industrial effort, the relative peace and prosperity of recent years, may have dulled the sense of the full demands of civic duty. We may forget that the powers of the platform, the Press, and the polling booth are derived from the conscious resolve of the people to maintain their rights and liberties. From time immemorial, it has been held by every race of mankind to be the right and duty of a freeman to defend his freedom with all his resources and with his life itself. The exercise of that right distinguishes the freeman from the serf, the discharge of that duty distinguishes him from the coward.

To drill, to learn the use of arms, to acquire the habit of concerted and disciplined action, to form a citizen army from a population now at the mercy of almost any organised aggression —this, beyond all doubt, is a program that appeals to all Ireland, but especially to young Ireland. We begin at once in Dublin, and we are confident that the movement will be taken up without delay all over the country. Public opinion has already and quite spontaneously formed itself into an eager desire for the establishment of the Irish Volunteers.

The object proposed for the Irish Volunteers is to secure and maintain the rights and liberties common to all the people of Ireland. Their duties will be defensive and protective, and they will not contemplate either aggression or domination. Their ranks are open to all able-bodied Irishmen without distinction of creed, politics or social grade. Means will be found whereby Irishmen unable to serve as ordinary Volunteers will be enabled to aid the Volunteer forces in various capacities. There will also be work for women to do, and there are signs that the women of Ireland, true to their record, are especially enthusiastic for the success of the Irish Volunteers.

We propose for the Volunteers' organisation the widest possible basis. Without any other association or classification, the Volunteers will be enrolled according to the district in which they live. As soon as it is found feasible, the district sections will be called upon to join in making provision for the general administration and discipline, and for united co-operation. The provisional Committee which has acted up to the present will continue to offer its services until an elective body is formed to replace it.

A proportion of time spared, not from work, but from pleasure and recreation, a voluntary adoption of discipline, a purpose firmly and steadily carried through, will renew the vitality of the Nation. Even that degree of self-discipline will bring back to every town, village, and countryside a consciousness that has long been forbidden them—the sense of freemen who have fitted themselves to defend the cause of freedom.

In the name of National Unity, of National Dignity, of National and Individual Liberty, of Manly Citizenship, we appeal to our countrymen to recognise and accept without hesitation the opportunity that has been granted them to join the ranks of the Irish Volunteers, and to make the movement now begun not unworthy of the historic title which it has adopted.

Original Manifesto of the Irish Volunteers distributed at the meeting held at the City Hall, Cork on 14 December 1914
[Courtesy of Cork Archives Institute]

Introduction

After dinner on Palm Sunday 1916 Seán O'Hegarty, a senior officer in the Cork Brigade of Irish Volunteers, met with Tomás MacCurtain and Terence MacSwiney, his commanding officer and second-in-command, at Tuirndubh near Ballingeary in West Cork. It was at this point O'Hegarty first discovered there was 'something on' the following Sunday. The Cork Brigade was to mobilise and march to selected locations all over the county to receive a shipment of arms that was scheduled to come ashore in County Kerry. Volunteers from the city companies were to go to Macroom, and then march north to occupy the high ground that dominated the Millstreet road. O'Hegarty was to move the Ballingeary Company to Kealkill, rendezvous with the Bantry Company, and having taken command of both wait until four o'clock in the afternoon when Peadar O'Hourihane would arrive from Cork on a motorbike with the latest intelligence update and orders to commence operations. Then, the Volunteers would go to war, launching a two-phased operation to capture the local police barracks before blocking and holding the Pass of Keimeneigh.

While it is generally accepted that military plans never survive first contact with the enemy this plan did not even reach the start-line. O'Hegarty spent the afternoon waiting for O'Hourihane who failed to arrive and eventually stood down his men. Then on Easter Monday at about one o'clock in the afternoon MacCurtain and MacSwiney arrived at O'Hegarty's home at Insemor, Ballingeary, and told him what they knew.

It transpired there had been a series of conflicting orders issued by both elements within the leadership of the Volunteer Movement – the IRB on one side and Eoin MacNeill on the other. This had been going on all week and culminated on Good Friday when the Military Committee of the IRB ordered that military operations would commence on Easter Sunday, only for MacNeill to issue further orders cancelling all mobilisation.

The situation had become impossible, and to make matters worse the shipment of German arms which Sir Roger Casement had been expected to land from the *Aud* was now lying beneath 150 feet of water a mile and half 'due south from Roche's Point, thus ensuring that any prospect of mounting successful operations in the south was effectively scuttled.

However, what none of them knew was that the situation nationwide was about to get infinitely worse before it got better and the Cork Brigade of Irish Volunteers would find itself almost disbanded before a resurgence of interest and patriotism saved it from extinction. But the interesting question that Easter Monday evening was not what the future held for the Volunteers but rather how this trio of officers, and many others like them, had actually come together in common cause in the first place.

Ultimately the Volunteer movement would survive and evolve into Ireland's constitutionally based Defence Forces. The founding fathers would receive public acclaim on 25 November 2003, the ninetieth anniversary of their organisation's birth, when two Irish government ministers, a host of civic and military dignitaries, and the British military attaché to Ireland gathered on the streets of Dublin to commemorate their historic achievement. But the formation the Cork Brigade of Irish Volunteers remained largely forgotten, with those who had the courage of their convictions to establish that unit barely receiving any recognition.

In association with Cork Public Museum, and drawing extensively on archival material available within Cork city and county, this book sets out to rectify that historical deficiency and regenerate interest in the Cork Volunteers amongst new generations of Irish men and women.

In 1913 Cork city was hopelessly divided on political lines, but those who passionately believed in the Volunteer ethos found it possible to identify common ground and then tread a difficult path to the eventual creation of a credible, competent and efficient local military organisation. By any yardstick one cares to employ their achievement was truly remarkable.

This is their story.

Origins

In 1800 the British government passed the Act of Union, which abolished the Irish parliament and replaced it with Irish representation at Westminster. This legislation came into effect on 1 January 1801 and in the years that followed the restoration of self-government, or 'Home Rule' for Ireland, became the primary objective of Irish constitutional nationalists. This issue soon developed a momentum of its own and came to dominate political debate in both Britain and Ireland after William Gladstone introduced his Home Rule Bill in the House of Commons on 8 April 1886. However, the bill failed to gain the necessary majority, and while the Commons passed the second Home Rule Bill of 1893, it was subsequently vetoed by the House of Lords.

Home Rule again came to the fore during the constitutional crisis of 1910–11 when attempts were made by Herbert Asquith's minority Liberal government to reform the House of Lords. This resulted in a situation where, in order to implement his reform package, Asquith found himself dependent on the votes of Irish Parliamentary Party led by John Redmond.[1] Passage of the subsequent Parliament Act of 1911 removed the power of veto from the Lords, and paved the way in *quid pro quo* fashion for the successful introduction of a third Home Rule Bill in the House of Commons on 11 April 1912. This time the Irish Party expected the bill to be on the statute books within two years.

While the majority nationalist population of Ireland welcomed this development, it met with fierce opposition from Ulster unionists led by Edward Carson and the country was plunged into crisis. The situation deteriorated further on 28 September 1912 when over 250,000 people gathered at Belfast's City Hall and signed a 'Solemn League and Covenant' pledging to resist Home Rule, with some even signing in their own blood. Then, in January 1913 the Ulster Volunteer Force (UVF) was formed with the specific objective of resisting Home Rule by force of arms if necessary. This organisation was led by ex-British army officers, and supported financially by businessmen and the landed gentry, and within months it was able to claim a membership of nearly 100,000 men.

Monitoring these events closely, the majority of nationalists became seriously alarmed, and none more so than the leadership of the Irish Republican Brotherhood (IRB), a secret oath-bound organisation founded in Dublin on 17 March 1858 by James Stephens. The IRB, together with the 'Fenians', its American auxiliary organisation formed in New York city on the same day by John O'Mahony, were dedicated to establishing an independent Irish Republic by force of arms. After the failure of the 1867 Fenian rebellion these organisations channelled their combined efforts into supporting both the Home Rule Movement and The Land

League and though numbers had declined by the 1890s the IRB still retained substantial influence as a result of its policy of infiltrating other nationalist bodies such as the Gaelic Athletic Association (GAA)[2] and Gaelic League.[3]

In 1898 the centenary celebrations of the 1798 Rebellion caused renewed interest in the IRB and led to an influx of young recruits, one of whom was Bulmer Hobson, a Quaker born in 1883 in County Down who joined the organisation in 1904. Hobson was also a member of the Gaelic League and in 1905 he founded Fianna Éireann, the republican youth movement, in Belfast. By 1913 he had risen to become a member of the Supreme Council of the IRB, and in the wake of the formation of the UVF he formed the opinion that the time had come to organise a similar Volunteer organisation in the south – although he knew that the IRB could not overtly play any part in it. Instead he decided to seek out a respected figure in Irish society to become the focal point for the new movement. Within weeks one emerged – Eoin MacNeill, Professor of Early and Medieval Irish History at University College Dublin, and a founding member and vice president of the Gaelic League. In his article, 'The North Began', published in the Gaelic League's journal, *An Claidheamh Soluis (The Sword of Light)* on 1 November 1913, MacNeill welcomed the advent of the UVF:

> There is nothing to prevent the other twenty-eight counties from calling into existence citizen forces to hold Ireland 'for the Empire'. It was precisely with this object that the Volunteers of 1782 were enrolled, and they became an instrument of establishing self-government and Irish prosperity.

Hobson first discussed the matter with The O'Rahilly, a fellow member of the Gaelic League and assistant editor of *An Claidheamh Soluis*, and together they approached MacNeill presenting a plan for the creation of a Volunteer force in the south. 'I had no doubt that both these men came to me from the old physical force party whose organisation was the IRB,' MacNeill later wrote. 'I also had little doubt of the part I was expected to play'.[4]

On Tuesday 11 November 1913 a meeting was convened at Wynn's Hotel, in Lower Abbey Street, Dublin. In attendance were MacNeill, Hobson, The O'Rahilly, Pádraig Pearse, Seán MacDermott, Eamon Ceannt, Seán Fitzgibbon, Piaras Beaslaí, Joseph Campbell, James Deakin and W. J. Ryan. With the exception of the last three, those present agreed to constitute themselves as a 'Provisional Committee', charged with the formation of an Irish Volunteer force. At subsequent meetings additional personnel were added until the committee totalled thirty people, and on 20 November, a letter was circulated to various national organisa-

Eoin MacNeill
[Courtesy of Cork Public Museum]

tions outlining the objectives of the new movement. Their stated primary goal was to 'secure and maintain the rights and liberties common to the whole people of Ireland'.

A public meeting to formally establish the Irish Volunteers was called for the Rotunda Rink in Dublin at 8 p.m. on 25 November 1913 and a crowd of over 7,000 tried to gain admission. Addressing the 4,000 people who crammed into the building, MacNeill presided over the meeting and declared:

> We are meeting in public in order to proceed at once to the enrolment and organisation of a national force of Volunteers. We believe that the national instinct of the people and their reasoned opinion has been steadily forming itself for some time past in favour of this undertaking. All that is now needed is to create a suitable opportunity, to make a beginning, and from a public meeting of the most unrestricted and representative kind in the capital of the country, to invite all the able-bodied men of Ireland to form themselves into a united and disciplined body of freemen prepared to secure and maintain the rights and liberties common to all the people of Ireland.[5]

Poster advertising the inaugural meeting of the Irish Volunteers
[Courtesy of Cork Public Museum]

Pádraig Pearse also spoke, and informed the crowd that:

> the bearing of arms is not only the proudest right of citizenship, but it is the most essential duty, because the ability to enjoy the other rights and to discharge the other duties of citizenship can only be guarded by the ability to defend citizenship'.

Addressing the on-going Home Rule debate he went on to say:

> there are people in the hall who share the belief that for Ireland there can be no true freedom within the British Empire. There are, doubtless, many more who believe that Ireland can achieve and enjoy very substantial freedom within the Empire. But Ireland armed will, at any rate, make a better bargain with the Empire than Ireland unarmed.[6]

Additional speakers led by Seán MacDermott relayed their message to those gathered outside the Rotunda. With the speeches finished stewards then mingled amongst both crowds distributing enrolment forms and in excess of 3,000 adult males enlisted. Among those who joined the Volunteers that night was Diarmuid L. Fawsitt, the secretary of the Cork Industrial Development Association (IDA).

Diarmuid Fawsitt
[Courtesy of Cork Public Museum]

He was also inducted into the IRB by Bulmer Hobson and immediately encouraged to explore the possibility of forming a body of Volunteers on his return to Cork city.

Originally founded as a monastic settlement by Saint Fin Barre around the year 606 AD, Cork first became known as 'The Rebel City' in November 1491 when its citizens gave their support to Perkin Warbeck, a native of Tournai. Warbeck declared himself to be 'Richard of York', the second son of King Edward IV and one of the young princes believed to have been murdered in the Tower of London by King Richard III. While his attempt to gain the throne of England was unsuccessful, and the pretender to the throne was hanged at Tyburn in 1499, a tradition of rebellion had been established amongst the citizens of Cork. This manifested itself again and again over the next 400 years, most noticeably in 1601 when the city magistrates refused to recognise the accession of King James I, in 1688 when Cork supported King James II in the wake of the 'Glorious Revolution', and in 1867 when over 2,000 Corkmen took part in the unsuccessful Fenian Rising.

However, during the nineteenth century the majority of nationalists in Cork believed that constitutional politics would best serve their ambitions and by 1840 many began to follow the Repeal Association founded by Daniel O'Connell. In 1873 the focus of political support was Isaac Butt's new Home Rule League which evolved into the Irish Parliamentary Party in 1882.[7] Three years later the Irish Parliamentary Party found itself in a pivotal position holding the balance of power in the House of Commons. During this period Charles Stewart Parnell represented the city in parliament[8] but in the wake of a bitter split in December 1890 the Irish Party broke into different factions.[9] It re-united under the leadership of John Redmond in 1900 after the formation and rapid rise of the United Irish League which was founded in 1898 by William O'Brien.[10]

O'Brien was an ardent advocate of policies based on what he called 'conciliation' and 'conference' in relation to both land re-

John Redmond
[Courtesy of Cork Public Museum]

form and Home Rule. He further believed that neither issue could be resolved without the prior unification of nationalists and unionists. However, the leadership of the Irish Party had a different view and at a public meeting in Cork City Hall, on 31 March 1910, O'Brien formed the All-for-Ireland League (AFIL) adopting the motto of 'Conference, Conciliation, and Consent'. Support for the AFIL was strongest in Cork city and county and in the general election of November 1910 O'Brien won eight seats sparking off bitter animosity between the two camps.

The Ancient Order of Hibernians (AOH) was also active in Cork at that time but it too had split into two distinct groups.[11] The majority known as the 'Board of Erin' (BOE) supported Redmond, while the minority known as the 'American Alliance' for the most part supported O'Brien. The nationalist political divide in Cork even extended to the city's brass bands as the writer Frank O'Connor later recalled:

> The Blackpool Band was an O'Brienite group, and our policy was 'Conciliation and Consent', whatever that meant. The Redmond supporters we called Molly Maguires, and I have forgotten what their policy was – if they had one. Our national anthem was 'God Save Ireland' and theirs 'A Nation Once Again' I was often filled with pity for the poor degraded children of the Molly Maguires, who paraded through the streets singing (to the tune of 'John Brown's Body'): 'we'll Hang William O'Brien on a Sour Apple Tree.' Sometimes passion overcame me till I got a tin can of my own and paraded up and down, singing: 'we'll hang Johnny Redmond on a Sour Apple Tree.[12]

Hostility between rival nationalist groups frequently erupted in almost open warfare with faction fights breaking out at public gatherings and formal meetings. The fights were fuelled by the fact that each political party also had its own newspaper which kept the momentum going with the *Cork Examiner* supporting Redmond and O'Brien's *Cork Free Press* advocating his policies. The other major newspaper in Cork at that time, the *Cork Constitution* put forward the views of the city's minority unionist population.

While the Irish Party and All-for-Ireland League provided a base for those in Cork wishing to pursue nationalist agendas by constitutional means, the more extreme separatists also had their own cultural and political groups. Many activists and agitators belonged to more than one of these

Cork Free Press
[Courtesy of Cork Public Museum]

disparate organisations. By 1900 both the GAA and the Gaelic League had also established branches in Cork city and county and that same year Arthur Griffith[13] and William Rooney[14] established Cumann na nGaedheal as a co-ordinating body for smaller societies who opposed English influences in Ireland. The 'Cork Literary Society', formed at a meeting on 2 January 1902 at No. 3 Marlboro Street,[15] and the Cork branch of the ladies society, Inghinidhe na hÉireann,[16] were both affiliated to Cumann na nGaedheal. The city also had an active branch of the 'National Council' – a body formed by the executive of Cumann na nGaedheal to protest against the visit to Ireland of King Edward VII in 1903.

In 1905 Arthur Griffith merged Cumann na nGaedheal and the National Council with the Dungannon Clubs to form a new separatist political party called Sinn Féin and on 3 December 1906 he addressed a public meeting at Cork City Hall and successfully called for the creation of a Cork branch of the party.[17] Although disagreeing with Griffith's policy of advocating a dual monarchy for Britain and Ireland, radical separatists in Cork gave the new organisation their support because at that time it represented the only political grouping publicly advocating independence from Britain. The following year separatists within the city formed a new a new branch of the Gaelic League known as the 'O'Growney Branch' which was located in Dun na nGaedheal in Queen Street (now Father Matthew Street) and the secretary of the new branch was Seán O'Hegarty who by 1910 had also become chairman of the Cork city branch of the National Council of Sinn Féin.[18]

Griffith's policies came under close scrutiny during O'Hegarty's chairmanship and in May 1910 the national policy of the party and the question of the effectiveness of the Cork branch became a matter of intense discussion. The debate culminated in vote on a motion calling for the abolition of the branch, which resulted in a tie and the issue was deferred to the following year. Dissatisfaction over party policies in the Cork branch continued and was exacerbated by the fact that the *Sinn Féin* journal had been commenting on parliamentary proceedings in the House of Commons. Many members felt this subverted the fundamental policies of the party and when the vote to discontinue as a branch of the party was taken in 1911 it was only defeated by one vote. On foot of this O'Hegarty and other republicans left the branch, and without its most effective members it soon became extinct, leaving the Irish Party and the AFIL to compete for the nationalist vote in the city.

This was the bitterly divided political landscape that faced Diarmuid Fawsitt when he returned to Cork after the euphoria of inaugural meeting of the Irish Volunteers in November 1913. Establishing a unit of Volunteers in the city would be no easy task and seeking someone of like mind to further the initiative he turned to James J. Walsh, a clerical officer

Seán O'Hegarty
[Courtesy of Cork Public Museum]

in the General Post Office who was also at that time chairman of the Cork County Board of the GAA. Walsh enthusiastically embraced the idea and wrote immediately to Eoin MacNeill asking him to address a public meeting in the city and on 3 December Fawsitt wrote to Liam de Róiste, a travelling commerce teacher employed by the County Cork Vocational Educational Committee and a prominent member of the Gaelic League, informing him:

> J. J. Walsh and myself have been discussing the Volunteer Movement. J. J. has extracted a promise from Eoin MacNeill to come to Cork and address the initial meeting. We propose having a further chat at 3 o'clock on Friday afternoon next, the 5th inst. for which we decided to invite Prof. Merriman and yourself along. Let me know tomorrow if the hour and day will suit you. J. J. Walsh is to ascertain the same from Prof. M.[19]

De Róiste was in favour of the Irish Volunteers and gladly accepted Fawsitt's invitation. He later described the mood at that time:

> The country was undoubtedly ripe for the idea. Dublin had only begun when a few of us were discussing the thing seriously in Cork. I felt, and I know others felt with me, that the thing was to be started by a few men, that all the Irish Nationalists ought to combine to make the beginning and work the idea to a success. 'An Irish Volunteer Army' – the very idea was appealing. 'To defend the rights and liberties of Ireland' – that was the object. The Tory party in England and the enemies of Irish Freedom had appealed to force – could Ireland not reply by force? Certainly yes.

J. J. Walsh
[Courtesy of Cork Public Museum]

Letter written by Diarmuid Fawsitt to Liam de Róiste inviting him to a meeting to discuss the formation of a Cork Corps of Irish Volunteers
[Courtesy of Cork Archives Institute]

Liam de Róiste
[Courtesy of Cork Public Museum]

Having denounced Carson's tactics as bluff, and being tied to a 'constitutional' and 'moral force' programme we felt that Mr Redmond and the chief men of the Irish Parliamentary Party could not well countenance a Volunteer movement, but that such a movement independent of them would be of the greatest benefit to their cause; and if they failed owing to the machinations of the English politicians, well, the Volunteers, an armed force, would be there to see justice done to Ireland.[20]

In the an effort to embrace all shades of nationalist opinion, Maurice O'Connor, a law student at University College Cork and well known member of the Ancient Order of Hibernians was also contacted and invited to attend. De Róiste also contacted a representative from the All-for Ireland League:

> I wrote to a prominent O'Brienite Co. Councillor whom I believed to be a good nationalist and an independent minded man and who I thought would have influence amongst men outside his own party, asking him to take some steps to set things going in Cork. His reply, full of party bias, and bitterness astonished me. I expected better of him.[21]

The first formal discussion went ahead after hours in the secretary's room of the Cork Industrial Development Authority offices at 28 Marlboro Street with only Walsh, de Róiste, O'Connor and Fawsitt in attendance.[22] It was at this point that a decision was taken to hold a public meeting in order to establish a 'Cork City Corps of Irish Volunteers' as Walsh later recalled:

> I was Chairman of the Cork County Board GAA at the time and it was arranged ... that I would preside at the City Hall meeting. J. L. Fawsitt would read the manifesto issued by the Dublin Provisional Committee and Liam de Róiste would propose a vote of thanks to MacNeill who was to be the principle speaker. Party political feeling was then very bitter between the Redmondites and the O'Brienites in Cork. We had the alternatives of having no speakers identified with either of the rival parties or, of inviting one from each side to speak. We wished to emphasise the non party character of the [Volunteer] movement so we decided to invite Eamon O'Neill from Kinsale as one identified in the public mind with the O'Brienite party, and John J. Horgan from Cork as one identified with the Redmondites, to attend and speak at the meeting.[23]

Admission tickets were then printed on green and white paper and distributed in bundles to GAA Clubs, Gaelic League Branches and every nationalist society and organisation in the city and neighbourhood.

On the Friday before the meeting it was discovered that Sir Roger Casement, the retired British diplomat and humanitarian who had embraced the cause of

Leanfam Go Dluth Do Chlu Ar Sinnsir
IRISH VOLUNTEERS

———————

Ticket of Admission to
PUBLIC MEETING
To be held at 8.30 o'clock, in the
CITY HALL, CORK,
On Sunday night next, 14th December, 1913
To Form a Cork City Corps of the
IRISH VOLUNTEERS.
Professor Eoin MacNeill, B.A., Dublin, and Local
Speakers will address the Meeting.
Volunteers embrace men of all Creeds, Classes, and Parties.
Only Citizens ready to join should attend, as the capacity of hall
is limited to 1,500.

J. J. Walsh (G.A.A.),
Liam De Róiste (Gaelic League)
Diarmuid Fasait (I.D.A.)
Maurice O'Connor (U.C.C.)

Muscail Do Mhisneach A Bhanba

Irish freedom, would be in Cork in an attempt to persuade the Hamburg-Amerika Line to have their ships call at Queenstown (Cobh).[24] He was immediately contacted and accepted an invitation to speak.

De Róiste was aware of the possibility that not all nationalist bodies in Cork would welcome the arrival of the Volunteers in Cork. He recorded in his diary that at some of the committee meetings he had warned of the possibility of disturbances at the public meeting and recommended that the necessary preparations be made. Walsh was of a different mind and waved all such warnings aside.[25]

However, by the Saturday night before the meeting it was evident that de Róiste's concerns were justified. He was informed by the Ancient Order of Hibernians (Board of Erin) that they would have nothing to do with the meeting because an advertisement had been placed in the *Evening Echo* by its rival, the Ancient Order of Hibernians (American Alliance), calling on its members to attend.[26]

Nevertheless, the following morning de Róiste and O'Connor went to the Great Southern and Western Railway Station on the Lower Glanmire Road to meet Eoin MacNeill only to discover that he had arrived on an earlier train.[27] When they eventually caught up with him MacNeill was already at the Imperial Hotel discussing plans for the meeting with Casement and John J. Horgan, whom, as de Róiste recorded in his diary:

Sir Roger Casement
[Courtesy of Cork Public Museum]

Cork City Hall 1910
[Courtesy of Cork Public Museum]

expressed sympathy with the Volunteer movement and on a word from MacNeill he was quite willing to speak from our platform that night, but as he was a member of the National Directory of the United Irish League and very prominently identified with the Redmondite party in Cork, he thought he may in some way compromise that party or compromise us with other parties should he come to speak.[28]

Many members of the Irish Party were also willing to support the new movement, but reluctant to do so openly without prior authority from Redmond who had not expressed any view on the matter. Prior to the meeting in City Hall Horgan wrote to John Muldoon, an Irish Party MP for Cork, asking him what course of action Redmond was recommending:

> Time was short and I asked him to wire Redmond's decision in code. If we should support the new movement he was to wire 'Deliver the books,' if otherwise, the reverse. A reply duly arrived containing the enigmatic message 'Deliver the books with care.' This we rightly construed to mean an instruction not to commit ourselves publicly.[29]

Horgan decided to follow these instructions and remain in the background while advising MacNeill as required. He later wrote that during their talk at the Imperial, MacNeill had informed him that he intended to call 'three cheers for Carson' at the meeting because he believed Carson was the man who had brought a new courage to Ireland.[30] Horgan said that while he totally understood where MacNeill was coming from many supporters of the Irish Party would be in the audience and would certainly misinterpret his intention. They would see such a call as being in line with O'Brien's policies of conciliation – which they vehemently opposed.

The organisers spent the rest of the day making final preparations for the meeting before accompanying MacNeill and Casement down the South Mall to City Hall. De Róiste, however, had a sense of foreboding and noted in his diary that 'I jokingly took a stick with me, saying it might be useful'.[31] Amongst the first to arrive at City Hall that night was an extremist element from the Ancient Order of Hibernians (BOE) who occupied the first six rows of seats nearest the platform in defiance of their own leadership who had that morning ordered a boycott of the meeting.

The hall began to fill rapidly and as 8 o'clock approached the auditorium was packed to capacity. The gallery, side passages and the space at the end, were all occupied. It was so crowded that a dozen or so would-be Volunteers had already spilled onto the stage. Boys from Fianna Éireann wearing full uniform lined both sides of the platform. The atmosphere was alive with anticipation, and amongst the many nationalists and republicans in attendance were Tomás MacCurtain,[32] a member of the Irish Republican Brotherhood (IRB), and Terence MacSwiney,[33] a founding member of the Celtic Literary Society.[34]

At 8.30 p.m. the organisers and guest speakers walked out onto the platform. Fawsitt opened proceedings by reading the Manifesto of the Irish Volunteers that had been adopted at the inaugural meeting in Dublin. J. J. Walsh spoke next telling the crowd that Volunteer units had already been formed in Dublin, Galway, Kilkenny and Kerry and that it was now time to form one in Cork because 'Corkmen had never been lacking in the fight for Freedom or the fight for anything else', and the movement which they were now initiating would be 'the Movement of the Irish Nation'.[35]

With the atmosphere at fever pitch, Walsh introduced the guest speaker. 'The right and duty of National Defence applies to every free people in the world,' MacNeill began, 'and the only question which arises is whether you consider yourselves to be a free people or not'.[36] Then, and in spite of persistent interruptions from one member of the audience seated in the gallery, he went on to explain the inequity whereby all other nationalities within the United Kingdom could join their own territorial force – except the Irish.

Referring to the formation of the Ulster Volunteers, and to a similar meeting of potential Irish Volunteers he had addressed in Galway the previous Wednesday, MacNeill informed the audience that he had 'particularly noticed at that meeting the manner in which young Galwegians, staunch Irishmen all, had stood up and cheered for Sir Edward Carson's Volunteers when he had mentioned them'.[37] This remark led to 'boos' and 'hisses' from some members of the audience and cries of 'we're not for England' from the gallery.

However, MacNeill continued speaking about the Ulster Volunteers calling them the 'descendants of the United Irishmen, of the men of 1798, and of those Ulstermen who had laid down their lives at Antrim and Ballynahinch.'[38] These remarks led one member of the audience to shout 'We will meet them half way'. MacNeill replied, 'yes, we *will* meet them half way, and when we do meet them it will be with open hands. It is they who have broken the ice for our ship to pass through. It is they who have opened the way for us. It is they who have set the model and public duty for us. We stand in no fear of them and they stand in no fear of us. There is no reason why either of us should fear the other.'[39]

Sitting on the platform, and observing the mood of the crowd, it was obvious to de Róiste that MacNeill's conciliatory remarks about the Ulster Volunteers were having completely the opposite effect on some of his listeners:

> He went on and on about it, laboured it till I felt he was making a mistake, a big mistake for a Cork audience where there were men who hated Wm. O'Brien and his conciliation policy, and to whom anything, no matter how patriotic, and no matter by whom put, that hinted at what they thought was O'Brienism, was anathema.[40]

De Róiste was correct in his assessment. MacNeill's message was being received with outrage by the Hibernians gathered in front of the platform who began to shout vociferously. When Walsh eventually managed to regain some order, MacNeill continued in the same vein telling the audience that 'the action of the Ulster Volunteers, interpret it as you will, is the very essence of nationalism. They have declared that whatever English political parties might say, they intend to have it their own way in their own country, and that is the definition of nationalism'. He then concluded by declaring 'the North began, the North held on, God bless Northern Ireland.' And raising his hand into the air, he cried, 'I will ask you to do as the young men of Galway did – Catholics and Nationalists – give three cheers for Sir Edward Carson's Volunteers!'[41]

This proved too much for the Hibernians, and Fawsitt described what happened next:

> There were scenes of indescribable chaos ... a portion of the audience became maniacs and shouts of 'get down', 'sit down' and 'get away out of that' were heard on all sides from the body in the City Hall and its gallery. It was like 'bedlam let loose'. The chairman (J. J. Walsh) rose to appeal for 'order' but his words were drowned in the noise and shouting. Professor MacNeill however, continued standing on the front of the stage gazing at the crowd of angry faces in the front seats. They threateningly turned towards him, then there was a cry of 'charge' from a prominent man in the front seat and a tossing sea of heads rushed towards the stage platform. The feeble efforts of those on the platform to stem the rush were abortive, and a howling crowd of angry men swept on, led by a town councillor of the Cork Corporation. Their attention was directed to Prof. MacNeill who was soon surrounded by a hostile mob. Every moment the number of protesters on the platform was augmented from the front seats of the hall, and when J. J. Walsh, as chairman, rose to attempt to halt this disturbance he was rushed upon. One incandescent protester lifted a chair and crashed it down on the chairman's uncovered head. His fall was the signal for a loud outburst of cheering and counter cries of 'shame'. Then the platform became as a congested boxing ring. Fierce fights were the order over the prostrate body of the chairman whose head was bleeding profusely ... One invader seized the water bottle from the chairman's table and would

have done tremendous damage had he not been struck under the chin by a pro-meeting man and sent sprawling on the stage to the accompaniment of the crash of broken glass.[42]

While many of those potential Volunteers who had earlier spilled onto the stage quickly fled the onslaught, those who remained put up what Walsh described as a 'stout resistance'.[43] De Róiste stood his ground and found himself surrounded by a crowd of angry Hibernians:

> Men wild, and angry, jumped up waving sticks and hats in the air. A rush at MacNeill, a rush at the chairman. I was in the midst of the wildest; one raising a stick shouting loudly for John Redmond. I spoke to him, to calm him, no use. He only shouted the louder. But I saw at once that I was in no danger – Walsh was the object of the attack.[44]

As the fighting continued, someone turned off the lights thus enabling the speakers to leave the platform under cover of darkness. This led many to believe that the meeting had been abandoned and rumour began to circulate that members of the Royal Irish Constabulary (RIC) were also gathered outside which quickly encouraged the trouble-makers to flee, demolishing many tables and chairs, and scattering the speakers' notes as they left.

Having survived the initial onslaught, de Róiste became concerned for the safety of the boys of the Fianna and availed of the cessation in hostilities to usher them safely from the hall:

> I went near one of the side doors and kept it open till the boys passed me. Then I descended to the dressing-room, got my hat and coat in the belief that the meeting was at an end. The stick that I had brought for protection I could not find! Next I was in the midst of a crowd in one of the passages. Sir Roger Casement, MacNeill, etc. There I heard that Walsh had been injured, struck on the head with a chair and carried off to the infirmary. Maurice Conway came to me and said there was still a big crowd in the hall; that the lights were on again; that if I got up on the platform I would be listened to. I answered as I believed right, 'not just yet; things should quieten down a little more'. Then I knew the meeting was not going to break up in disorder. I crossed to another side passage. I met some men there, 'cornerboys' – who demanded money for drink. 'Hangers-on' of the Redmondite crowd I knew them to be. To get them away I, perhaps weakly, gave them some money.[45]

Once the Hibernians had left the hall the lights were turned on again and the speakers began returning to the platform hoping to resume the meeting. While the newspaper reporters had departed believing the meeting to be over, a large crowd still remained in the hall. Fawsitt then climbed onto one of the few remaining undamaged chairs and asking the crowd to resume their seats called on Casement to come forward. Still standing on his chair, he placed his left hand on Casement's right shoulder and told the crowd, 'Here is a man who would be welcomed warmly in every Chancellery in Europe. Will Rebel Cork deny him a hearing?'[46] This plea was greeted with loud applause. De Róiste later wrote that Fawsitt had saved the day:

Fawsitt was listened to quietly and applauded. Then Casement. He caught the crowd. One could see he was a man of the world, one who had travelled, who had mixed up with varied people. Tall, supple, commanding, he looked every inch a man.[47]

For his part, Casement assured the crowd that the Volunteer movement had his fullest sympathy and support and said that he felt the meeting had not fully understood the sentiments expressed by MacNeill. He then said he had received a letter from Colonel Maurice Moore,[48] the son of the politician George Moore[49] expressing 'delight and approval that a Volunteer movement was afoot'.[50] Casement then said that Colonel Moore hoped to see a large body of Volunteers on parade at the nine-hundredth anniversary of the Battle of Clontarf. He concluded by describing Ireland as a 'mother' whose sons should unite to protect her, just like Wolfe Tone, Thomas Davis and Michael Dwyer had already done.

Anxious to capitalise on the momentum of the meeting Maurice Conway pushed de Róiste to the front of the platform urging him to thank Casement on behalf of the organising committee and then further explain the purpose of the meeting to the audience:

> Fawsitt, eager to catch a train, asked me to be short, I was, but he had to go before I was finished. I respectfully asked that the organisers of the meeting be given authority to form a Provisional Committee to go on with the organisation of the Volunteer corps in the city. This was given with acclamation. We had wanted to have a committee definitely named, the appointment of which was to be submitted at the meeting. Owing to the 'row' this had to be abandoned, as it was quite likely that some of the men named would not act. But I had not forgotten that it would be necessary to get public authority to go on with the work, and we got it. I concluded with a few lines from the poem of Brian Higgins which winds up as follows, 'Awake, arise, be men today'.
>
> As I concluded in that burst of applause that well-chosen verse always evokes, up jumped an old Fenian who was near the platform (stage I should say) and handed me the form of enrolment which he had filled. That was the opening for others, up they came; trooping in tens, in twenties, singly, in batches. I had my overcoat on. Into every pocket I 'stuffed' the forms. It was marvellous. Old men, boys in their teens; up they came. It was thrilling. There were a few hundred, I said so amidst a thunder of applause. Then the audience went out. There was a small crowd on the stage. Phil O'Neill of Kinsale mounted a chair and sang a Volunteer song he had composed for the occasion. We cheered him. Then we left. We had won. The Volunteers were a living reality in Cork.[51]

In excess of 500 men had put their names on the enrolment forms and for these new Volunteers it was a night to remember.[52] As they left the City Hall and made their way home in the cold night air many were jubilant and proud of their achievement in having joined the movement. Among the new recruits was Liam Ruiseal who later recorded that a number of supporters had escorted Roger Casement to Turner's Hotel, singing, 'Rory of the Gael' to the air of 'The Boys of Wexford' as they made they way triumphantly through the streets.[53]

The following morning newspaper reports of the meeting focused primarily on the violence which had erupted giving the clear impression that the meeting had leanpam ʒo ʋlúṫ ʋo ċlú áṗ ṗinnṗiṗ.

Company...................... No......|......

óʒlaiʒ na héineann—**Irish Volunteers.**

I, the undersigned, desire to be enrolled in the Irish Volunteers, formed to secure and maintain the rights and liberties common to all the people of Ireland without distinction of creed, class, or politics.

Name........ *John   Ahern*

Address........ *39th Kellahan Buildings*

Date........ *Ashburton*

Corcoran, Printer, 21, Sullivan's Quay, Cork.

First application for membership of the Cork City Corps of Irish Volunteers distributed at the City Hall on 14 December 1914
[Courtesy of Cork Archives Institute]

ended in disorder. On his way to early mass de Róiste encountered a placard for the *Cork Constitution* which ran the headline' 'Scores involved in bloodshed at the City Hall' and he later penned a short reply, giving the facts of what had occurred after the reporters left.[54]

MacNeill also wrote to the press to clarify his position and Monday's *Cork Examiner* published his letter in which he stated that 'a number of the audience understood me to ask for cheers for Sir Edward Carson. This would amount to an endorsement of Sir Edward Carson's present policy which is far from my mind'.[55] Tuesday's *Cork Examiner* carried a letter from someone calling himself 'Common Sense' who identified three of the organisers of the Cork meeting as those who express the 'extreme', or Sinn Féin brand, of nationalism. He also suggested 'those really interested in the Movement had better ensure that it is not used like the "All-for-William" League, as a weapon to hit the Irish Party and the Home Rule cause'. The letter concluded by condemning the Sinn Féin party claiming that 'their ideas of organisation and business methods are as crazy as their politics'.[56]

Public debate continued in the *Cork Examiner* and on Thursday the Irish Party MP Richard Hazleton wrote that, 'Having been asked by some of my constituents whether I think they would be acting wisely in the interests of the national cause joining the new departure called the Irish Volunteers I felt bound to tell them that, in my opinion they would not'. Referring to MacNeill's attempt to raise a cheer for the Ulster Volunteers he said:

Is it not a little premature to set up Sir Edward Carson and 'Galloper' Smith as models to rank with the heroes of Dungarvan? We have yet to learn that the leaders of the Ulster Volunteers and their movement stand for aught but bigotry, intolerance, reaction, minority domination and British misrule, riveted upon us ... And when we are told that the right way to meet this danger is to cheer for Sir Edward Carson and follow the hideous example he has set, I refuse to agree. If the 'Irish Volunteers' were started to resist the 'Ulster Volunteers' on their threatened march to Cork, it would be a case of meeting bluff with ridicule; but when they are started to 'welcome' them on their way to Cork it is a case of meeting bluff with lunacy.[57]

The same edition of the paper carried a copy of correspondence sent to the *Irish Times* by Eoin MacNeill giving his account of the events at City Hall and in which he responded to an earlier editorial contained in that paper:

My personal politics have been a private concern until now, but since you have set me down in your editorial as belonging to the Sinn Féin party, you have made it incumbent on me to say publicly that I am, and have long been, a supporter of Mr John Redmond.[58]

Notwithstanding the intense political debate which greeted their formation that December, the Cork City Corps of the Irish Volunteers had been born and, as J. J. Walsh was later to write, it had been 'baptised in blood'.[59]

2

Expansion

Having successfully established the Cork City Corps, the organisers next turned their attention to the mundane matters of administration and logistics with the first, and most important, matter being the question of who would lead the unit. Accepting that one of the fundamental principles to under-pin the entire Volunteer movement would be democracy, it followed that each unit would elect their own leaders.

However, before any election could be held it was necessary to constitute a 'Provisional Committee' to administer the unit and those who assembled in the City Hall had already mandated the organisers to form such a group. Accordingly, all shades of nationalist and republican political opinion gathered together under the chairmanship of J. J. Walsh, with Fawsitt as vice-chairman, Tomás MacCurtain honorary secretary and Liam de Róiste honorary treasurer. The other members were: Maurice O'Connor; Seán O'Hegarty; Terence MacSwiney; Maurice Conway (representing O'Brienite interests); Denis O'Mahony (a former member of the Cork Literary Society and a Redmond supporter); Seán Jennings and Diarmuid O'Donovan (both members of the AOH); Seán O'Cuill (a member of the Gaelic League); Liam Owen and Daniel Enright (both students at UCC); and Seán O'Sullivan and Patrick Corkery, of whom de Róiste would later write:

> they were young men ready to do or die for Ireland, differing much in opinion, differing often in ways and means of doing things, but all held together by one desire – to serve Ireland; with one idea – to make our Volunteer corps a success.[1]

It was also decided to assemble the new corps at 'An Dún' on Queen Street at 8 p.m. on Friday, 19 December and all who had signed enrolment forms in City Hall were invited to attend – but only 150 men turned up. Undeterred, the committee resolved to continue parading at 'An Dún' three nights per week and fixed a weekly subscription rate of three pence (3d.) per man to finance activities. Tomás MacCurtain had secured the services of Bill Goodwin, a former artillery sergeant major in the British army, and he immediately commenced instruction in the rudiments of foot drill. Goodwin was unable to attend parades on a regular basis but John Donovan, a former sergeant in the Dublin Fusiliers, whom de Róiste described as 'a better instructor than Goodwin [and] one of the best teachers I had known', made himself available as an instructor. Thereafter individual, squad, and section drill was taught on a regular basis.

It quickly emerged that because the rooms available at 'An Dún' were all upstairs and very small, the scope and scale of training was severely restricted. The committee decided to approach the Munster & Leinster Bank on the South Mall and a loan was approved. This enabled the Volunteers to begin the new year by

Óglaiġ na h-Éiрean.

IRISH NATIONAL VOLUNTEERS.

THE IRISH NATIONAL VOLUNTEERS have been organised to defend the rights and liberties of the Irish Nation.

These rights and liberties, in defence of which some of the best men of our Nation gave their lives, and for the maintenance of which this Nation has struggled for centuries, are threatened openly by one of the great English political parties, the leaders of which declare that if they are returned to power in England they will use all the available force at their command to check the National aspirations of the Irish people, to crush the liberties and the rights of the Irish Nation.

One of the first duties of the citizens of any nation is to arm for the defence of the nation against aggression; the armed citizen connotes the free citizen; the armed nation makes the free nation possible. Tyrannical governments have, in all ages, disarmed the peoples they wished to hold in slavery. As the world is constituted to-day, the disarmed nation is a nation in bondage; the unarmed peoples are the subject peoples.

No nation can afford to have the defence of its rights and liberties permanently delegated to a specially hired military organisation. It is incumbent upon every man who is able to defend the rights and liberties of his nation. Hence none but the Irish people themselves can guard the rights and liberties of Ireland. It is their duty to themselves and to their country to arm and train for defence, as it should be their pleasure and their pride to do so.

The last degree of Irish national degradation will be reached if the Irish Nation, which holds a record for valour, for courage, for military prowess and achievement second to none of the nations of Europe will have to depend upon a foreign soldiery to defend it from outside aggression or maintain peace within itself.

The National Volunteer movement is not aggressive but defensive. The Volunteers seek no quarrel, but, if properly maintained and supported by the Irish people, they will be the surest guarantee the nation can have against any possible future tyranny, and the best support for the permanence and free action of a Home Government.

The training and discipline incidental to a Volunteer force are bound to have a moral effect of the greatest advantage to the nation. Men's minds will be imbued with a true conception of citizenship, of patriotism, of duty, of self-sacrifice, of self-control, of order, steadiness, sobriety and courage. Discipline is the first principle of an army; obedience the first duty of a soldier—virtues that help men to the higher life.

The Irish National Volunteers, while drawing recruits from all sections of the Irish people, and seeking the co-operation of all, will be identified with none. Their mission is a national, not a sectional one.

Young men wishing to join the Cork City Corps are invited to call to the Headquarters, Fisher Street, off St. Patrick Street, any night between 8.30 and 10.30.

March, 1914.

Recruiting pamphlet distributed in March 1914
[Courtesy of Cork Archives Institute]

moving to a new home at 19 Fisher Street where the initial rental was set at £20.00 for six months. It was now possible to man the headquarters on a daily basis and the premises functioned both as a recruiting office and a training centre.

The fate of the fledgling organisation improved dramatically on 3 April when Cork Corporation granted the Volunteers the use of the city's Cornmarket for training. The leadership then issued a new organisational training plan which provided for the creation of a 'Cork City Battalion', comprising eight companies of 100 men each. Formed 'by district' the companies were expected to train on two nights per week at either the Cornmarket or Fisher Street, with the whole battalion detailed to parade at the Cornmarket every Sunday morning. Route marches were planned for Wednesday afternoons, Friday nights and Sunday mornings while company and section commanders, and additional drill instructors were appointed. Each company also had to elect delegates to attend battalion meetings, with three such persons attending each night at Fisher Street, and a further two reporting on Sundays to the Cornmarket. Additionally, individual Volunteers were issued with numbered membership cards which recorded their weekly subscriptions, and before long sentries appeared on guard duty each night at Fisher Street. However, it was acquisition of the Cornmarket as a training installation which proved critical to the formation of the new organisation. It was from here, two days after it had been handed over by the corporation, that over 100 Volunteers, led by a solitary piper and uniformed members of Fianna Éireann, set out on their first field-training exercise – a route march from Cork to Blarney. One of the Volunteers who took part in that first outing was Patrick Sarsfield (P. S.) O'Hegarty:

> It was a curious experience that march. Outside the Cornmarket the street was lined with people, and, as we swung out, very conscious of ourselves and wondering what we looked like, there was almost dead silence from the people. One or two who began to titter were roughly threatened by a tough citizen, but for the most part there was just silence, silence and a sort of wistful curiosity. Many of those who looked on, I felt, would have liked to march with us, but they did not want to 'make a show' of themselves. And yet they must have felt something of the magic of the moment. And it was the same through the city. All along the route people stopped and lined the streets and gazed at us, neither approving or hostile, but just wondering, with something vague stirring far back in their consciousness. It was a wet day, but we never minded, and when 'Stand at ease' was given by Tom Curtain halfway to Blarney, we felt that we had been baptised, that we were almost soldiers. After that the march became steady and confident. And at Blarney right opposite the police station, we held a recruiting meeting at which Terry [MacSwiney] spoke. And then back again. As we walked into Cork it was dark, and the curious could not see us, [they] could only hear the tramp, tramp and see the bulk of marching men. But as we tramped down Blarney Street we

P. S. O'Hegarty
[Courtesy of Cork Public Museum]

The Cork City Corps of Irish Volunteers on parade in the Cornmarket on Sunday 5 April 1914 prior to their route march to Blarney
[Courtesy of Cork Public Museum]

met a priest coming up. And he stopped, took off his hat, and said: 'God Bless ye boys anyway'. And so we swung home and we dismissed.[2]

That march enhanced the standing of the Cork City Corps and training excursions into the countryside continued on a regular basis, although not everyone in the city welcomed their arrival. In fact J. J. Walsh later recalled that the Volunteers were regularly 'stoned by the citizens' as they set off on manoeuvres.[3] Nevertheless, unconcerned by either missiles or taunts, the Volunteers continued training and slowly began to transform themselves from civilians into soldiers.

Inspired by the meeting in the Rotunda Rink and acting on their own initiative, prominent nationalists and republicans in other parts of Cork county had also formed Volunteer companies in their own districts. Michael Leahy, who was then one of three members of the IRB in Cobh, gave this account of the formation of his Volunteer Company:[4]

Immediately after the public meeting for the formation of the Volunteers in Dublin in November 1913, and before the public meeting in the City Hall Cork ... a group of us who were attending a Gaelic League class in a room in the A.O.H. Hall, Cobh, decided to hold a meeting to form a Volunteer corps. We held the first meeting in the Gaelic League room in the A.O.H. Hall without asking any permission from the A.O.H. authorities. About 25 attended the meeting, and all were men who were attending the Gaelic League class. Liam Murphy acted as secretary for the first meeting, and I acted as secretary for some time afterwards ...

It was decided to send a deputation to wait on the A.O.H. committee and ask for permission to use the Gaelic League Room for drilling on nights when the Gaelic League was not using it for classes. I was one of the deputation. Joseph Healy was chairman of the A.O.H., and he told us that while he himself thought the Volunteer movement a good thing, Mr Redmond had made no pronouncement about it, and pending that we could not have the use of the room. We then applied to the Urban Council, and that body gave us the use of a field near the town. An ex-naval man, Warrant Officer Downey, who was an enthusiastic Gaelic Leaguer started drilling us. We had about 25 at that public parade. A large crowd looked on and jeered. That parade had been held before the public meeting in the City Hall, Cork, and when Cork started I attended the City Hall meeting and put our group in touch with the Cork committee.[5]

Captain Cornelius Meaney
[Courtesy of Tom Meaney]

The men who formed new Volunteer companies in Cork county during this period represented all shades of nationalist opinion. Thomas J. Golden, of Gurrane, Donoughmore (who later became a battalion commandant) recalled the formation of the Courtbrack Company:

> In December 1913 a company of Volunteers was started in the Courtbrack chapel area which covered portions of the parishes of Blarney, Donoughmore, and Inniscarra. The majority of the members of the company and those in control were Redmondite supporters and those of us in the area who were not Irish Party followers did not join at first, though some efforts were made to induce us. [However] about May 1914 a number of us joined the company in response to an appeal for recruits.[6]

Cornelius Meaney a member of the IRB from Carriganimma provided this account of the formation of the Volunteers in Millstreet where party loyalties initially led to two separate units being formed during the days before and after the county council elections of June 1914:

> The A.O.H. party, in preparation for an election victory which they did not achieve, formed a branch of the Irish Volunteers, but they did not affiliate with headquarters. This Volunteer company was under the charge of an ex-NCO of the British army, who put them through some close order drill and short route marches. They were armed with dummy wooden guns.
>
> On the night of the declaration of the election results the victory of [Dan Linehan], the O'Brienite candidate was announced. The town of Millstreet was thronged with supporters of both parties. A large force of RIC stood ready to use their batons. The A.O.H. Volunteers assembled at the A.O.H. headquarters on the square, fell in and proceeded to march to the West End. The RIC cleared a path through the angry O'Brienites. When the marchers passed clear of the throng there were subdued cries of 'Get them on the return boys'. At this juncture Jerry Twomey and I, who were standing on the sidewalk, stepped into the centre of the O'Brienite crowd and reasoned with those who advised an attack on their political opponents. At our suggestion this group, overt 100 strong, formed fours and proceeded in processional order in the direction taken by the A.O.H. men An ex-British soldier took charge. About midway between the square and the West End both bodies of marchers met. Each got the order, 'Left incline', and then, 'Eyes right' and that ended the feud between the Redmondites and the O'Brienites in Millstreet.
>
> That night the O'Brienites decided to meet a few nights afterwards. At the next meeting a corps of Irish Volunteers was formed with a strength of approximately 120 men. A civilian was formed and the corps was duly affiliated to headquarters.[7]

'Dummy' rifle used to train members of the Irish Volunteers in arms drill
[Courtesy of Cork Public Museum]

THE IRISH VOLUNTEER

THE RIGHT TO MURDER!

ENGLAND'S CLAIM.

Ireland's Protest against the Arms Proclamation and England's Answer

The English Government, through the Executive responsible to it, has reasserted its old claim—the right to murder the Irish people without even the formality of a trial.

Bullet and bayonet, rope and poison, were the instruments by which English law was enforced for centuries, and if of late years they were not in use it is not because they were superseded, but because they were held in abeyance for the generation that would question the slaves heritage. Active as instruments or hidden from sight as a menace they were ever ready to fulfil their purpose—to keep the Irish people a race of helots.

Men and women of Ireland—there are stark corpses to-day in Dublin, there are widows and orphans in the streets of Ireland's Capital. Why? Let justice answer if British justice that invests

Issue of The Irish Volunteer
[Courtesy of Cork Public Museum]

Ammunition bandolier worn by the Irish Volunteers
[Courtesy of Cork Public Museum]

While new Volunteer companies were being formed throughout the county, in Dublin things were moving on as well. In April 1914, a woman's organisation called Cumann na mBan was formed and it functioned as an auxiliary body for the Irish Volunteers. The movement also had its own journal, *The Irish Volunteer*, edited by Lawrence de Lacey, which contained articles on military tactics, and was used to keep the membership up to date with new regulations and instructions. The Provisional Committee had by now established a headquarters in Dublin, at 206 Great Brunswick Street, and took responsibility for all matters affecting the movement.

From its inception, the founding figures considered the movement to be the nucleus of a new national army and the Provisional Committee quickly recognised the need to be publicly identified and defined as such. While initially new recruits paraded in neat civilian attire, with some wearing brown leather bandoliers and carrying white haversacks, it was obvious from the outset that this was not consistent with their image of what soldiers of an Irish army should look like.

Accordingly, early in 1914 a uniform sub-committee was appointed to identify an appropriate Volunteer uniform and in their report submitted on 12 August they found:

> that no suitable uniform cloth was made in Ireland. They therefore obtained samples of high class uniform serge from a well known English Mill. From these they selected a Grey Green cloth of a very suitable colour for field work in Ireland. They then inquired from several Irish mills whether they could and would match this sample. The business was not keenly sought after as the mills were full of orders and the extent of the Volunteers' requirements was somewhat uncertain. Finally Messrs. Morrogh Bros of Douglas Mills, Cork got special looms working and matched the sample. The sample they sent was submitted to experts and pronounced excellent. It was therefore decided to give the first order to Morrogh Bros.[8]

The sub-committee also addressed the matter of uniform design and it was agreed that all ranks and units would wear a standard tunic with rolled collar, dark green shoulder straps and pointed cuffs complete with brass buttons bearing an Irish harp and the letters 'I.V.'. Breeches and puttees of light serge that matched the tunic would also be worn as would a brown leather waist-belt fastened by a round brass clasp bearing the words 'Óglaigh na hÉireann' the inscription that was later emblazoned on the standard Volunteer cap-badge designed by Eoin MacNeill and worn by all units. Head-dress would consist of a round crowned cap with a black patent leather peak and chin strap similar in design to that worn at the time by the Cossacks in Russia. With regard to head-dress, the report stated that while it had been 'decided upon for the Dublin regiment it was left undecided for the other regiments with a considerable body of opinion favouring soft hats'.[9] A soft hat, similar in pattern to that worn by the Boers in South Africa was later selected for 'field work' and became known as the 'Cronje Cap' – so called after the Boer General Piet Cronje.

Irish Volunteer officer pattern tunic
[Courtesy of Cork Public Museum]

Once Morrogh Bros. produced the cloth an initial order for the manufacture of 300 uniforms was placed with the Limerick Clothing Factory of Lower Bridge Street in Dublin. However in its report the sub-committee found it necessary to note that notwithstanding these arrangements:

'Cronje Cap' belonging to Terence MacSwiney
[Courtesy of Cork Public Museum]

> numbers of Volunteers obtained uniforms elsewhere than from the official supplies and in many cases these uniforms were not of standard material or standard design. It had been decided that as the Volunteers were a democratic force all uniforms should for the time be exactly similar. No distinction was made between officers and others as all officers were purely temporary. Notwithstanding this several Volunteers seem to have got uniforms designed as officers uniforms.[10]

On further investigation the sub-committee discovered that:

> owing to delays of various kinds Morrogh Bros., who had stocked the cloth, [then] disposed of some of it to various traders who started making and advertising all kinds of

Belt buckle worn by members of the
Cork City Corps of Irish Volunteers
[Courtesy of Cork Public Museum]

uniforms' – and advised that in future all uniform orders should be sent through the sub-committee.[11]

In spite of the best efforts of the Provisional Committee in Dublin, the Volunteers did not have the luxury of a quartermaster's stores from which to draw their kit and all were still expected to purchase their own uniform and accoutrements. Not surprisingly then the cut and colour of uniforms tended to vary greatly as local tailors often had to work without a pattern and use cloth that didn't precisely match the approved colour. The same applied to buttons and belt buckles, many of which were made locally, and this accounted for the somewhat diverse appearance of the Volunteers in the early days of the movement.

Volunteer headquarters in Dublin dealt with administration of the movement at national level while local commanding officers dealt with the day-to-day operation of their respective units. As the summer of 1914 approached the Cork City Corps was still without an officer with sufficient military experience to train the unit to a high level of military proficiency. In May 1914 Capt. Maurice Talbot Crosbie, a retired British army artillery officer from Ardfert, County Kerry, who was then living in Monkstown and working with the Trinidad Lake Asphalt Company on Albert Quay in Cork, wrote to Liam de Róiste expressing interest in the Volunteers. On 21 May De Róiste replied setting out the objectives of the movement and inviting him to attend the Cornmarket drill on Sunday, 24 May. Crosbie accepted this invitation and on that Sunday he enlisted in the corps, but because of his previous military experience he was elected commanding officer.

The Provisional Committee in Cork had always envisaged the city and county companies would ultimately become one single formation and as the movement grew it soon became obvious that all of these new formations could not function without a clearly delineated chain of command. With Capt. Crosbie taking control of the military functions of the Corps J. J. Walsh was able to devote his time to improving the organisational structure in the remainder of the county. He was ideally suited to this task because his position as chairman of the Cork GAA County Board provided him with an intimate knowledge of the countryside and brought him into contact with many other key nationalists and republicans. He later recalled the challenge of this task with great pride:

Capt. Talbot Crosbie
[Courtesy Irish Examiner]

Having made a start in the City Hall, my next job was to organise the county. This proved easier, and the only barrier that I could not surmount was that Party hatred engendered by the political split. As a consequence, I was faced with rival corps everywhere, and were it not for the fact that Capt. Talbot Crosbie … who by the way possessed a motor car, accompanied me, progress would not have been easy … Our first run was to West Cork, which included such towns as Bandon, Dunmanway, Bantry Skibbereen and Clonakilty. At Bandon we were met by Seán Hales and his men from Ballinadee … At Bantry there was the unique spectacle of no less than three potential armies. At the entrance we met and addressed the O'Brienites. In the middle of the great square were a few Sinn Féiners. While at the other end we addressed the Redmondites. It was a tiring experience, but compensation was in store in Skibbereen where we were played into the town by a brass bands that had recently been presented by that generous citizen, Macaura, of Pulsicon fame. Later Mr Macaura treated us to a magnificent banquet in the West Cork Hotel. At midnight we reviewed the Volunteers of Clonakilty. Incidentally I was dressed on that occasion in the first Volunteer uniform worn in this Volunteer movement. It happened this way The O'Rahilly had given an order to Messrs Mahony of Blarney for the grey-green cloth. The Mahony firm which I knew very well, obliged me with a length which I had made into a uniform by that old established concern of T. Lyons and Co. The first appearance of the new garment created something akin to a sensation.[12]

While the Volunteer movement continued to expand numerically during the early months of 1914 two significant events occurred which had major political repercussions throughout Ireland. On 14 March, in an effort to strengthen security in Ulster before the enactment of the Home Rule Bill, the War Office instructed the commander of British forces in Ireland, General Sir Arthur Paget, to prepare plans for the protection of arms depots. Paget was informed that while officers residing in Ulster would not be expected to act in their own area, all other officers based in Ireland would be required to carry out their orders or face dismissal.

On 21 March Brigadier General Sir Herbert Gough, the officer commanding 3rd Cavalry Brigade based in the Curragh, telegraphed the War Office informing them that together with fifty-seven of his officers he would accept dismissal rather than take action against Ulster. Faced with a mutinous situation the British government backed down and Gough was assured that under no circumstances would he, or his officers, be used to enforce Home Rule in Ulster. This incident, which became known as 'The Curragh Mutiny', eventually resulted in the resignation of the Chief of the Imperial General Staff, Field Marshall Sir John French; the Adjutant General, Sir Spencer Ewart; and the Secretary of State for War, Colonel John Seely.

Encouraged by the success of the 'Mutiny' the leadership of the UVF then staged a major political and military coup. On 24–25 April a cargo of 35,000 rifles and five million rounds of ammunition, purchased in Germany, were successfully landed at Larne without any interference from the security forces – in open defiance of the British government's proclamation on 5 December 1913 prohibiting the importation of arms into Ireland. Overnight, the UVF became a force to be reckoned with, and speaking in the House of Commons on the following day, Sir Edward Carson accepted full responsibility for the operation but no action was taken against him.

Reaction amongst nationalists was immediate with hundreds of new recruits rushing to enlist in the Irish Volunteers. With its strength standing at 27,000 nationwide (6,000 of whom had signed up in Cork) numbers began to rise dramatically. Unlike the UVF who enjoyed substantial support within the British military and political establishments, the Irish Volunteers remained politically isolated because John Redmond still viewed the entire movement with deep suspicion.

Eoin MacNeill was unhappy with this situation and on 26 April he embarked on negotiations with Redmond to secure his support. While some prominent Volunteers, such as Bulmer Hobson and Casement, were aware of MacNeill's activities the matter was not discussed within the Provisional Committee. MacNeill was seen to be acting in a personal capacity, with no official authority or approval,

Óglaiġ na h-Éirean.

IRISH VOLUNTEERS. CORK CORPS.

Headquarters: FISHER STREET,
CORK, June, 1914.

THE IRISH VOLUNTEERS are no longer a mere proposal. They are a living reality. Their call to arms has been answered by tens of thousands of young Irishmen in every part of Ireland. Irishmen everywhere have laid aside their differences and come together on the common meeting-ground for all Irishmen—a National Army.

The Volunteers are the nucleus of a permanent defence force. If properly maintained, they will form a National Army; such a force as has not been in Ireland since the great days of Grattan. So far, no call for financial help has been made to the Irish people—at whose service the Volunteers are—to equip their own army. The expenses of the Organisation have been met by the small subscriptions willingly given, in many cases at a sacrifice, by those enrolled. But to procure equipment for this army of the people, it is necessary to appeal to the people, and the Provisional Committee in Cork now appeals with confidence to the citizens for financial aid.

To make clear the magnitude of the task, it should be borne in mind that a full equipment, uniform and all arms, would cost approximately £10 a man. It is evident that exceptional sacrifices are called for. The Volunteers themselves are conscious of this, and an urgent appeal has been addressed to the men individually. This has met with a generous response. The members are subscribing, in addition to their weekly subscription, to a special fund for equipment. It is hoped our wealthy citizens will come forward with sums which are not small. In little Ulster towns humble people have raised large amounts for the Ulster Volunteers, while in many cases wealthy Ulstermen have subscribed sums of £10,000. It will be to our eternal discredit if we are less ready to meet the demands of the National Volunteers.

Finally, a National Army is our best National investment. It will restore our prestige as a Nation; and by the security it provides for the powers we shall acquire, it will give stability to our commerce and confidence to our people.

Any one of the signatories to this appeal is authorised to accept subscriptions. Cheques and money orders may be made payable to either of the Treasurers and crossed to the Munster & Leinster Bank "For the Irish Volunteer Fund."

(Signed)   MAURICE TALBOT CROSBIE, Commanding Cork Corps.
J. J. WALSH, T.C., Chairman of Provisional Committee.
DENIS O'MAHONY, T.C., Vice-Chairman   ,,
LIAM DE ROISTE }
JOHN JENNINGS } Hon. Treasurers.
T. MAC CURTAIN, Hon. Secretary.
MAURICE CONWAY.
J. L. FAWSITT.

Appeal for funds issued by the Cork Corps, Irish Volunteers in June 1914
[Courtesy of Cork Archives Institute]

and many committee members feared that if Redmond came on board his supporters would then attempt to take total control of the movement.

It was also clear that keeping the nationalist lobby divided served no purpose, and with hundreds of recruits rushing to join the new movement on a weekly basis Redmond also came to realise that it wasn't within his power or interests to waste time trying to change things. In early May he let it be known the he had no further objections to his supporters joining the Volunteer Movement and on 18 May the Central Executive of the AOH also instructed all its members to co-operate with the Volunteers.

Redmond had always made it clear that he considered the Provisional Committee to be self-elected and unrepresentative of the wider nationalist opinion and to address this issue MacNeill, on 9 May, persuaded the committee to announce plans for a national convention to be held in the autumn.[13] To prepare adequately for this event an instruction was issued to all Volunteer companies to affiliate with the Provisional Committee on or before 10 June. County conventions would then be held on 28–29 May to elect county representatives to sit on a new national executive.

In the meantime talks between MacNeill and Redmond continued focusing primarily on the formation of a small executive committee representative of both shades of nationalist opinion to run the movement. However, negotiations proved extremely difficult culminating in complete failure to find a compromise.[14] Responding to the breakdown, Redmond issued a letter to the press on 9 June stating that while he initially considered the arrival of the Volunteers to be 'somewhat premature' recent events had altered his position and it was desirable for all nationalists to support the movement. He nevertheless believed that the existing Provisional Committee was 'self-elected' and therefore should now be replaced by a new body representing all shades of nationalist opinion. To achieve this end he suggested that the existing Provisional Committee be augmented with twenty-five Irish Party nominees from different parts of the country claiming that 'the committee so reconstituted would enjoy the confidence of all nationalists'. In conclusion he said:

> If this suggestion is accepted, the National Party and I myself will be in a position to give our fullest support to the Volunteer movement, but failing the acceptance of some such arrangement as that above suggested I fear it will be necessary to fall back on county control and government until the organisation is sufficiently complete to make possible the election of a fully representative executive by the volunteers themselves.[15]

This proposal was designed to give Redmond control of the entire Volunteer movement and on the night of 9 June a meeting of the Provisional Committee was convened to discuss this matter and they decided to reject Redmond's suggestion and press ahead with their own plans for county representation. On hearing this Redmond responded in another letter to the national press which appeared on 13 June. He again accused the Provisional Committee of being 'self-constituted' and stated that while the majority on that body were not supporters of the Irish Party, 'of the rank and file at least 95 per cent are supporters of the Irish Party and its policies'. He then said that this was a 'condition of things which plainly cannot continue' and concluded by saying:

> I regret that the Provisional Committee should so hastily have come to a decision to repudiate my suggestion. It is of most vital importance to the national cause that this matter be settled in an amicable spirit, and without friction of any kind which would not be possible under the proposal made by the committee and unless the committee can see their way to reconsider their decision and adopt the proposal I have made I must appeal to all supporters of the Irish Party in the Volunteer movement to at once organise county committees quite independent of the Dublin Provisional Committee, and to make independent county government of the Volunteer movement until the organisation is sufficiently complete to make it possible to hold a representative convention to elect a permanent governing body which will have the full confidence of the country.[16]

Faced with this ultimatum the Provisional Committee convened an emergency meeting on 15 June to consider what action to take. After very heated debate, MacNeill stood up and proposed acceptance of Redmond's demand to avoid fragmentation of the entire movement. When the votes were counted eighteen had voted in favour with nine against. A statement issued by the Provisional Committee the following day declared that:

> The Committee recognises for the time, in view of the new situation created by Mr Redmond's attitude, it is no longer possible to preserve the unity of the Irish Volunteers and at the same time maintain the non-party and non sectarian principle of organisation which has hitherto been maintained, and which by securing the cordial support of national opinion has brought about the splendid spirit that pervades and invigorates the Volunteer Movement.
>
> This being the case, the Committee, under a deep and painful sense of responsibility, feel it their duty to accept the alternative which appears to them the lesser evil. In the interest of national unity, and in that interest only, the Provisional Committee now declares that, pending the creation of an elective Governing Body by a duly constituted Irish Volunteer convention, and in view of the situation clearly forced upon them, they accede to Mr Redmond's demand to add to their number twenty-five persons nominated at the instance of the Irish Party.[17]

In a letter to the press on 17 June those who had voted against the proposal stated that they had done so because they believed 'it was a violation of the basic principles which up to the present have carried the Volunteer movement to success'. Nevertheless they went on to declare that it was their:

> duty to continue our work in the movement; and at the same time we appeal to those of the rank and file who are in agreement with us on this point to sink their personal feelings and persist in their efforts to make the Irish Volunteers an efficient armed force.[18]

In the wake of this development the Provisional Committee in Cork decided to clarify their mandate at the ballot box. An election for a new executive committee was held on 21 June and all enlisted Volunteers, including new recruits, were allowed to vote. When the ballots were counted, a new Cork Executive Committee emerged bearing a marked resemblance to the one just stood down: Chairman, J. J. Walsh; Vice-Chairman, Denis O'Mahony; Honorary Treasurer, Liam de Róiste; Assistant Honorary Treasurer, Seán Jennings; Honorary Secretary, Tomás MacCurtain; Assistant Honorary Secretary, Seán O'Hegarty; together with Thomas Barry, Seán O'Cuill, Maurice Bulmer, J. P. Lane, Patrick Corkery, Diarmuid O'Donovan, Thomas Donovan, Tadgh Barry, Henry Lorton, Matthew Comerford, Tom Nash, Patrick Harris, Terence MacSwiney, Seán O'Sullivan and Maurice Conway as ordinary members.

This left Redmond's supporters in Cork totally dissatisfied and ready to consider forming their own unit. However Volunteer headquarters in Dublin acted immediately to avoid such fragmentation and directed that five Redmondites be co-opted on to the Cork Executive Committee. On 1 July the following personnel joined the committee: Patrick Ahern, Thomas Byrne, George Crosbie, J. F. O'Riordan and Capt. Maurice Talbot-Crosbie. Diarmuid Fawsitt was also added to the committee and later in the month when Thomas Nash resigned P. S. O'Hegarty was co-opted in his place, notwithstanding very strong attempts by the Redmond faction to have another of their own brought on board.[19]

Once the matter of the Executive Committee was settled a separate Military Council was then appointed which consisted of Tomás MacCurtain, Seán O'Hegarty, Seán O'Sullivan, Seán Murphy and Patrick Corkery. Of crucial significance here was the fact that while the Executive Committee had responsibility for all administrative and financial matters, the Military Council (now comprised entirely of people from the original Cork Provisional Committee) had successfully managed to retain control of the key areas of organisation and training.

Under MacCurtain's direction the new Military Council set about transforming the Volunteer organisation in Cork city. Four new company areas were established with the city divided north and south of a line running from Blackpool Bridge through Shandon Street, North and South Main Streets and Barrack Street, to the Bandon Road. The area west of this line and south of the southern arm of the River Lee was the A Company area. B Company was located east of the line and south of the river, while east of the line and north of the river was the C Company area, and west of the line and north of the river was D Company's territory.

The addition of Redmond's nominees to the executive brought in hundreds of Irish Party followers as new recruits and Volunteer units were soon formed in almost every town and parish in the county. This attracted favourable newspaper attention with the *Cork Examiner* reporting on 22 June:

Tomás MacCurtain
[Courtesy of Cork Public Museum]

A muster of the Cove (Cobh) National Volunteers took place here today in the fore-noon, previous to a route march to Ballymore village, some four miles distant. Considering the hilly nature of the country traversed, the Volunteers looked fit and well at the end, and were very much admired as they swung through the town at a good marching pace with the band at their head. With [when they have] rifles on their shoulders and uniforms to enhance their martial appearance, it is easy to conceive that they will be a valuable acquisition to whatever regiment of the National Volunteer army they will eventually be attached.[20]

On 4 July all Cork Volunteer companies paraded in review order at Mitchelstown before the newly appointed Volunteer inspector general, Colonel Maurice Moore. He said they were the best units he had reviewed thus far and three weeks later, on 25 July, the Executive Committee formally adopted two designs for their unit colours. The national colour consisted of a seven-stringed gold harp on a green background, and the regimental colour would be a representation of the Cork coat of arms on a blue background.[21]

While these developments were welcome, a fulltime organiser still had not yet been appointed for Cork county and members of the Executive Committee were bridging this deficiency by visiting the rural companies whenever they could. This was particularly true in MacCurtain's case who, notwithstanding his strenuous work-load as secretary of the Executive Committee and member of the Military Council, availed of every spare minute to establish and maintain contact with the officers and men of the 'country units'. On 11 July the Executive Committee announced that following instructions issued from Volunteer headquarters in Dublin, a county convention, consisting of delegates from all Volunteer companies in County Cork, would be held on 16 August to select a county delegate to attend the national convention in the autumn.

Irrespective of how well organised the Volunteer movement was at this time, it was still virtually powerless given its totally inadequate stocks of arms and ammunition. While some members, who could afford the expense, had gone ahead and commenced equipping themselves with hunting rifles and shot-guns, supplies of combat weapons were urgently needed for everyone else if the organisation was to be taken seriously. On 24 June the Provisional Committee in Dublin announced the establishment of the 'Defence of Ireland Fund' which would be opened for subscriptions in each Volunteer district from Sunday 12 July to Sunday 9 August. In a circular issued the Provisional Committee declared that 'the money subscribed to this fund will be directed solely to the purchase of arms and ammunition for the Volunteers [with] the equipment so purchased distributed among the various Volunteer companies in proportion to the amount they have collected or subscribed'.[22] In Cork the Volunteers established a special committee to deal with fund-raising and they opted for a church door collection. On 12 July Cork Volunteers positioned themselves outside all masses held in city and county and raised £60. A door to door collection followed, and was supplemented by individual subscriptions made by Volunteers themselves. Then on 31 July a public meeting was held in the City Hall under the auspices of the lord mayor Alderman Harry O'Shea to establish a public fund for the equipping of the Cork City Corps of Volunteers. These efforts were so successful that at the end of August the executive was able to send £600 to Volunteer headquarters – and another £100 to John Redmond.

The first effort to procure weapons actually came earlier in the year when Sir Roger Casement, on his own initiative, travelled to England and raised £1,500 to purchase a consignment of arms and ammunition. This money was then handed over to the London Volunteer committee who sent Darrell Figgis to Antwerp where he purchased 1,500 rifles and 45,000 rounds of ammunition which he loaded on a transport ship and then crossed-decked onto two small yachts in the middle of North Sea. Nine hundred rifles were loaded onto Erskine Childers' yacht, *Asgard*, with the remaining 600 stowed away on Conor O'Brien's smaller craft before both set sail on separate routes for Ireland. On the morning of Sunday 26 July, Childers arrived at Howth, Co. Dublin. Almost 800 Volunteers (twenty-five per cent of whom were armed with nothing more than wooden batons) turned out to

Notice issued by the Provisional Committee, Irish Volunteers on 24 June 1914 informing members about the Defence of Ireland Fund
[Courtesy of Cork Archives Institute]

unload the cargo having allayed RIC suspicions by pretending to have been up to nothing more revolutionary than a routine Sunday morning route march. Once the consignment was safely ashore individual Volunteers used bicycles and taxies

Postcard commemorating the arms landing at Howth, County Dublin on 26 July 1914
[Courtesy of Cork Public Museum]

to take them to safe locations in the city until they could be distributed. Although most of the Volunteers managed to reach their locations without interference, one group was stopped by British soldiers and RIC on the Malahide Road where, after a short scuffle, the Volunteers lost nineteen precious rifles. Nevertheless, the operation was a spectacular success, and when the remaining 600 weapons eventually came ashore at Kilcoole, County Wicklow on 1 August morale improved greatly.[23]

Morale also improved in Cork when the executive received fifty of the so-called 'Howth Rifles'. Twelve were later given to both the Ballinadee and Courtbrack Companies, while the Dunmanway Company got two and the Ballingeary Company one, leaving twenty-three for the city Volunteers.[24] These rifles enabled the Military Council to commence meaningful training that summer in the area of drill, discipline and marksmanship, even though ammunition was limited to one or two rounds

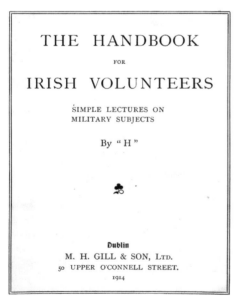

Irish Volunteer Handbook printed in 1914
[Courtesy of Cork Public Museum]

per weapon. Other aspects of military training continued at the same time with lectures on subjects such as tactics, map-reading and first aid, being given during week-night sessions. On Sundays the Volunteers were expected to partake in route marches and tactical exercises designed to improve fitness, develop individual field-craft skills and foster group cohesion.

By mid-August 1914 the leaders of the Cork Corps had much to pleased about. The unit was up and running with numbers increasing daily and training was ongoing. Fund-raising activities had commenced and a further shipment of weapons was expected via the Defence of Ireland Fund. Perhaps most importantly, preparations were in train for the county convention, which would strengthen contact between the Executive Committee headquartered in the city and the Volunteer companies scattered throughout the county.

However, before the convention could be held, events were under way elsewhere which would fragment the Cork Corps of Irish Volunteers in ways then unimaginable. The fragile unity, so carefully nurtured over the past six months, would soon be shattered by the outbreak of the First World War – and the knock-on effects it was destined to have in Ireland.

Irish Volunteer Pipe Band
Back Row: M. *Trahey, Donal Barrett, Martin Donovan, D. O'Gorman, Tadhg Hegarty*
Centre Row: *Seán O'Sullivan, N. Waters, M. McCarthy, D. Hurley,*
J. Courtney, James Hastings
Front: *Daniel Foley, Michael Wickham, Tadg Barry, William Horan, Louis Courtney,*
D. McCarthy, Patrick Horan
[Courtesy of Cork Public Museum]

3

Division

During the last week of July 1914, while the world watched the European powers slide towards war, the city of Cork was a hive of military activity. Detachments of soldiers from Victoria Barracks made their way daily through the city streets to take up defensive positions along the Cork coastline and armed RIC patrols were guarding all crossing points on the River Lee.

The Cork City Corps of Volunteers were also active that week and on Friday 31 July a public meeting was held in the City Hall to raise money to fully equip the unit. The lord mayor, Alderman Henry O'Shea, had called the meeting at the request of the Volunteer finance committee. J. J. Walsh, Seán Jennings, Maurice Conway, George Crosbie and J. F. O'Riordan attended from the Executive Committee, together with Capt. Talbot Crosbie, many city councillors, members of the clergy and a number of prominent citizens.

Informing the gathering of the meeting's purpose, the lord mayor declared that 'the Volunteers are a different organisation to anything else in the country because it is open to men of all classes and grades in politics, and that is why it is so much appreciated and meeting with such widespread support.'[1] Seán Jennings then informed the meeting that as matters currently stood the Cork Volunteers had a credit balance in the bank of £436-1s-0d and this money had been collected at church doors and in house-to-house collections. He also stated that among the many donations he had received was one for thirty shillings which came from a group calling themselves 'The Sympathisers', with an address care of 'The British Army, Cork Barracks'.[2]

J. J. Walsh spoke next outlining the needs of the unit and informed the meeting that as of that moment the Cork Corps of Volunteers had two regiments in training, with a third at a stage where they were almost ready to shoulder rifles. He said he eventually anticipated raising a corps of over 2,000 Volunteers and in his opinion approximately half of these would need some financial assistance to equip themselves. 'Those who joined the Volunteers,' he reminded the audience, 'have not done so for fun but from a sense of patriotic duty. They have made sacrifices, and they have pledged themselves to make even greater sacrifices should the time ever come for doing so.'[3] Walsh went on to say that somewhere between £4,000 to £5,000 would be required to fully equip the Cork Volunteer sub-units but he hoped that once this was complete the public would not be called upon to subscribe another penny for many a long day.

Once Walsh had finished the following motion was unanimously adopted by the meeting:

That this meeting of representative citizens, called together by the Lord Mayor, at the instigation of the governing committee of the Cork Volunteers, places on record its whole-hearted approval of the Volunteer movement as a potent step on the road to national liberty, and pledges itself to give every assistance possible.[4]

The meeting turned its attention to the appointment of treasurers for the fund which was to be established and the following resolution, proposed by Councillor T. C. Butterfield, was adopted by acclamation:

> That the following gentleman be appointed treasurers of the special Cork City Volunteers Fund hereby inaugurated – Capt. Talbot-Crosbie, Mr M. J. Nagle J.P., Mr John J. Horgan solr. H.C., Mr John Jennings and Mr Liam de Róiste, and that all monies received be lodged in the Munster and Leinster Bank, Ltd., in the names of the above treasurers, the monies so lodged to be used for the equipment of the Cork City Volunteers under the direction of the Volunteer Committee; and that those present constitute themselves a collection committee to assist the existing Volunteer Committee.'[5]

Having passed a motion of thanks to the lord mayor, the meeting, which had lasted about an hour, concluded with the fund established. A further £162 was added to the fund thanks to the generosity of some present who were sufficiently inspired by the occasion to make an immediate contribution.

Concurrently, rank and file Volunteers were getting on with more practical matters as they responded to a series of orders commanding all of the city companies to parade at the Cornmarket at 8 a.m. on the Bank Holiday Monday, 3 August. Once assembled the plan was to board a train at the Cork and Bandon Railway Station near City Hall, travel to Skibbereen, and then hold a special parade through the streets with a view to generating support for the movement (which was meeting with apathy from the bulk the town's people) and thereby encouraging new recruits to join. However, the main objective of the exercise was to facilitate collection of 3,500 Italian rifles which had been purchased by monies donated by individual Redmondite supporters and from the Defence of Ireland Fund, and which were due to arrive in Baltimore harbour on Sunday night.

But the storm clouds that had been gathering over Europe for months finally burst that Saturday when Germany declared war on Russia. On hearing the news Redmond immediately dispatched a telegram to Talbot Crosbie calling off the Baltimore operation because the ship carrying the arms had been intercepted by the British authorities and diverted to Dublin port where it was detained.[6] Talbot Crosbie sent a message to the railway station cancelling the train and when Volunteers assembled in the Cornmarket on Monday morning he informed them that the entire operation had been cancelled. He availed of the opportunity to offer his own opinion on the role of the Volunteers in the coming days and informed those on parade that in the event of Britain going to war he believed the Volunteers should provide military support to the war effort. He then ordered that a vote be taken to establish whether the Cork Corps should apply directly to the British government for a supply of arms, a move which greatly exceeded his actual authority as com-

Volunteers training at Cork Park in the summer of 1914 under the watchful eye of their commanding officer Captain Maurice Talbot Crosbie
[Courtesy of Cork Public Museum]

manding officer. It was highly improper of Talbot Crosbie to embark on this course of action without the approval of higher authority. After the parade the Executive Committee issued an order to all company commanders instructing them to inform the men under their commands that the vote was not binding on anyone and all offers to supply the unit with weapons, irrespective of where they came from, would be considered on their own individual merits.

The following morning, the *Cork Constitution* recorded that the railway station-master had treated Talbot Crosbie's cancellation of the train with deep suspicion, thinking it was what he called 'a base O'Brienite plot', and instead ordered that the train be prepared. This explains why when some Volunteers who had skipped parade, arrived at the railway station they found the Skibbereen train waiting and: 'A curious scene of cross purpose ensued until the leading spirits succeeded in explaining the case, and the assembled stalwarts, performing a flank movement, fell back in good order upon the Cork Park where some hours were profitably devoted to drills and evolutions.'[7]

The conflict was meanwhile escalating in Europe. Germany declared war on France on 3 August and issued an ultimatum to Belgium demanding that German forces be allowed complete freedom of movement throughout her territory. Based on treaty obligations to Belgium, Britain's entry into the war now seemed inevitable. As far as John Redmond was concerned the matter was clear, and addressing the House of Commons on 3 August he made an impassioned speech:

> In past times, when this Empire has been engaged in these terrible enterprises, it is true – it would be the utmost affectation and folly on my part to deny it – the sympathy of the nationalists of Ireland, for reasons to be found deep down in centuries of history, has been estranged from this country.

He went on to recall how at the end of the American War of Independence, when Britain's military power was at its lowest ebb, a body of 100,000 Irish Volunteers came into existence to defend Ireland but no Catholic had been permitted to enlist. Having caught the attention of the House, Redmond concluded by declaring:

> May history repeat itself today! There are in Ireland two large bodies of Volunteers.

One of them sprang into existence in the South. I say to the government that they may tomorrow withdraw every one of their troops from Ireland. I say that the coast of Ireland will be defended from foreign invasion by her armed sons, and for this purpose armed nationalist Catholics in the South will be only too glad to join arms with the armed Protestant Ulstermen in the North. Is it too much to hope that out of this situation there may spring a result which will be good, not merely for the Empire, but good for the future welfare and integrity of the Irish nation?[8]

The following day Britain declared war on Germany and Liam Ruiseal later described the mood in Ireland at the time:

With the outbreak of the First World War a tremendous wave of imperialism swept the country. Red, white and blue badges were worn everywhere, and were it not for a hard core of Gaelic League and Volunteer people, Irish-Ireland would have been swamped. Recruiting meetings, processions with bands, were regular features [used for] recruiting for the British army.[9]

Notwithstanding his censure by the Executive Committee, Talbot Crosbie, once again acting on his own, sent a telegram to the secretary of state for war offering him the services of the Cork Corps of Volunteers. He then ordered the city Volunteers to parade at the Cornmarket on the night of 4 August where he read out the official reply:

The Secretary of State desires me to convey to you his thanks for the patriotic offer of the Cork Corps of the Irish Volunteers of their services. He would gladly keep that offer in mind should the necessity arise.[10]

There was no indication of approval from the rank and file on parade and the following morning, the *Cork Constitution* recorded that:

it must be assumed that those on parade, numbering fully 500, had made up their minds to accept the new policy and guard the shores of Ireland should the necessity arise. It is well known that there are a small number of Irish Volunteers who are extreme Sinn Féiners, and supporters of the Gaelic revival, and who are sore that the Volunteers at the insistence of Mr Redmond should be prepared to accept arms or in fact anything else from the British Government; but it is expected that these will secede from the ranks or be overborne by moderation.[11]

The majority of the Executive Committee greeted this second public pronouncement with outrage and at a meeting on the night of 5 August they decided to put their own position before the people of Cork. Tomás MacCurtain was directed to write immediately to the press informing them that Talbot Crosbie's actions were unauthorised and should be disregarded while Liam de Róiste was to formally write to Talbot Crosbie asking him to explain his actions. The following resolution was then passed supporting a decision taken by Provisional Committee in Dublin to endorse Redmond's offer to use the Volunteer movement only for the defence of Ireland:

> That the committee of the Cork City Corps, Irish Volunteers, approve of the proposals set forward by the Provisional Committee, and are prepared to act in accordance with their recommendations, namely – that the Irish Volunteers are prepared to join with the Ulster Volunteers for the defence of Ireland.[12]

At this point relations between Talbot Crosbie and the remainder of the Executive Committee collapsed. The dispute then entered the public domain when his letter appeared in the *Cork Constitution* on 6 August:

> A vital point has been reached in the existence of the Irish Volunteers, and it is absolutely necessary to decide whether we are prepared to stand by the British Empire and come forward for the defence of Ireland against foreign aggression, or are not prepared to do so.
>
> Without raising any question of detail, which I consider to be of quite minor importance, I put the broad issue before the Cork City Corps on Monday morning, when they gave an answer in the affirmative.
>
> I have now been informed that the committee of the Cork City Corps desire to disassociate themselves from my action, and I have been asked by Mr Liam de Róiste, the treasurer, to give this statement publicity.
>
> Yours etc.
> M. Talbot Crosbie[13]

The day after the letter was published Talbot Crosbie's position within the Cork City Corps, and the Volunteer movement as a whole, was considerably strengthened when Colonel Maurice Moore, the Volunteer Inspector General, appointed him chief inspecting officer for County Cork.

The next morning, the position of the majority within the Executive Committee also became public when MacCurtain's letter appeared in the local newspapers:

> IRISH VOLUNTEERS CORK CORPS
>
> Sir – I am directed by the Executive Committee to say that recent references which have appeared in the local press with regard to matters of policy affecting the Cork Corps were unauthorised and should therefore, be disregarded.
>
> T. Mac Curtain
> Hon. Sec.[14]

The main problem now was that while still commanding a majority on the Executive Committee, Walsh and his supporters were aware that Talbot Crosbie could probably muster a majority of the rank and file in both city and county. This situation was highlighted by another letter published in the *Cork Constitution* on 8 August in which J. McGrath, a 'company commander', took issue with the Executive Committee's censure of Talbot Crosbie:

> I wish to inform the public that this action of the Cork City Corps committee does not

represent the attitude of the Cork City Volunteers seeing the almost unanimous response to Capt. Crosbie's question. There were nearly 1,000 Volunteers present on Monday and out of that number only three answered in the negative, so it is plain to be seen that the committee's action has not the approval of the rank and file. There are a few men at the head of this committee and I understand they were responsible for the 'vote of censure' on Capt. Crosbie. These gentlemen are called 'extreme' Sinn Féiners and I am of the opinion that the sooner they are removed from the committee the better it will be for the progress of the Volunteer Movement in Cork.[15]

Neither Walsh nor anyone else had any intention of resigning but rather than risk a complete fragmentation of the unit, they decided not to press the matter further for the moment. In any case there was sufficient distraction as news continued to emerge of the German army's march into France, and the people of Cork witnessed dramatic scenes of their own. British army reservists were called up all over the city and county and the first troops to leave for the war marched proudly from Victoria Barracks to the Great Southern and Western Railway Station on the Lower Glanmire Road. They were cheered off by family and friends, many of whom waved Union Jacks, sang 'Rule Britannia' or 'A Nation Once Again', and roared their cheers for 'King and Empire'.[16]

However, others of military age still believed their most patriotic course of action was to enlist in the Volunteers and letters poured into Fisher Street on a daily basis offering service and seeking additional information about the movement. In response to these enquiries Talbot Crosbie again wrote to the press, and having outlined the objectives of the movement, he made some conciliatory remarks:

We have no intention of altering our principles, and all Irishmen are welcomed into the organisation. The question of accepting Government assistance in arming, etc., is at present under consideration by the headquarters, Provisional Committee, and without instructions from them it is obviously impossible for the individual units to take any action in the matter. It is as well to say at once that the vast majority of the Irish Volunteers are nationalists; and, although we are perfectly willing to co-operate with our unionist fellow countrymen for the defence of our common country from foreign aggression, it must not be assumed that this indicates any weakening in our national aspirations.[17]

He also used the letter to postpone the county convention which had been planned for the following Sunday, and to publicise proposals for a new 'county organisation' based on twenty 'Battalion Districts' which would each have it's own management committee.

Walsh immediately responded to this olive branch by writing the following letter to the local press:

Sir – The unfounded idea seems to prevail that the local Volunteers have had differences recently. Loose talk of this kind can do no good. The situation reflected in Capt. Crosbie's letter of yesterday is correct in every detail, and is, as far as I know, in complete accord with the feelings of every Volunteer.

J. J. Walsh[18]

An uneasy peace then followed between Talbot Crosbie and his opponents on the Executive Committee and everyone turned their attention to matters of organisation and administration.

However peace of any description was far from the minds of those fighting on the continent during August as the German army pushed deep into French and Belgian territory and the first elements of the British Expeditionary Force (BEF) landed at Boulogne and Le Harve. Then, as the BEF prepared for battle, the British government turned its attention to both Volunteer movements in Ireland. It was obvious from the outset that the UVF would willingly supply manpower to the war-effort but the position of the Irish Volunteers was still unclear. To clarify this position Sir Arthur Paget met with Colonel Maurice Moore on 5 August and two days later Redmond met with the Secretary of State for War, Lord Kitchener, to discuss arming the Irish Volunteers. After these discussions, Asquith, on 10 August, told the House of Commons that Kitchener would 'do everything in his power, after consultation with gentlemen in Ireland, to arrange for the full equipment and organisation of the Irish Volunteers'.[19]

Six days later, having presented colours to the local corps of Volunteers at Maryborough, Queens County, Redmond declared:

> It will be possible for me very shortly, to distribute over several thousand rifles. In addition to that I have information to the effect that the government which is withdrawing its troops from Ireland, and which is refusing to send English territorials to take their place, and which has publicly declared through the mouth of the Prime Minister that it entrusts the defence of Ireland to the Irish Volunteers are about to arm, equip and drill a large number of Volunteers and with the rifles which my colleagues and I are about to supply, the rifles which are being supplied from various other quarters and with the rifles which will be supplied by the Government the day is near when I believe every Irish Volunteer will have a rifle in his possession.[20]

While this announcement met with approval from his own supporters, the Provisional Committee in Dublin issued a statement on 19 August denying the existence of any agreement which would permit the War Office to take control of the Volunteers movement. It did however reaffirm the willingness of the Irish Volunteers to join with their Ulster counterparts in defending Ireland in line with Redmond's original proposal in the House of Commons on 3 August.

Once again tension between Talbot Crosbie and the Executive Committee began to rise and came to a head on Friday, 28 August. The captain took issue with another article in the *Irish Volunteer*, and in response wrote a letter which appeared the following morning in the *Cork Constitution*:

> The Irish Volunteers
> Who is on the King's Side?
>
> Sir,
>
> It is an open secret that there has been for some time past considerable friction be-

tween different sections of the Volunteers, and a leading article in the current issue of *The Irish Volunteer,* the official mouthpiece of the Provisional Committee brings things to a head.

In this article it is boldly stated: 'England's war is not our war, except in so far as it offers Ireland a unique opportunity to achieve freedom' With this declaration before us it is necessary to ask where the Volunteers stand. Are we going to co-operate with the British troops, or are we going to follow the committee with its chimerical schemes for the establishment of an independent Irish republic.

Personally, as soon as the Home Rule Bill is placed on the Statute Book, I will be prepared to offer myself to the British Government for war service, and on this clear understanding, I will ask the Cork City Corps on the 12 o'clock parade next Sunday to choose between myself and their committee, the large majority of whom I have reason to know are in complete agreement with the Provisional Committee in Dublin.

It is time that things were clearly defined, for when the greatest war the world has ever seen is in progress, a soldier must know on what side he is fighting.

Some of us will be prepared to offer our services to fight the enemy wherever he is to be found; others will be content to wait passively until he gets the opportunity to land in this country. But this is really beside the point for the main question to answer is this: 'Are we prepared on the passage of the Home Rule Bill into law to co-operate with the British army, or are we not prepared to do so?'

As it is well known, the Volunteer movement was started by a few extremists who naturally obtained a firm hold on the different committees. After the movement had been in existence for some time, the Irish people suddenly had the fact forced upon them that the forces of the crown might, under certain circumstances, refuse to enforce the constitutional law of the land, and so nullify the political efforts of generations. The effect was instantaneous, and thousands of Irishmen joined the Volunteers. It is one thing, however, for a force to prepare itself to supply amateur policemen, a totally different thing for that force to supply men capable of contending with continental troops, and that is the position at the present moment. We must know where we stand, and the Cork City Corps must make their decision next Sunday.

	M. Talbot Crosbie,
August 28, 1914	Chief Inspecting Officer
Albert Quay, Cork	County Cork Irish Volunteers[21]

As far as the majority on the Executive Committee were concerned this was unacceptable. Talbot Crosbie had now firmly set out his position and a battle for the hearts and minds of the Cork Volunteers was about to begin. Time was now critical and Tomás MacCurtain called an emergency meeting of the Executive Committee for that Saturday night. He also sent a telegram, seeking instructions, to Eoin MacNeill who replied: 'With reference to letter of Talbot Crosbie in today's newspapers, questions regarding policy cannot be proposed by anybody to Volunteers on parade nor answered by them'.[22] Fortified by MacNeill's reply, the meeting of the Cork Executive Committee passed a resolution in Talbot Crosbie's absence: 'The committee cannot countenance and will not allow any address to the men on matters of policy'.[23] It also decided to take immediate action to regain complete control of the movement in Cork by passing a second resolution:

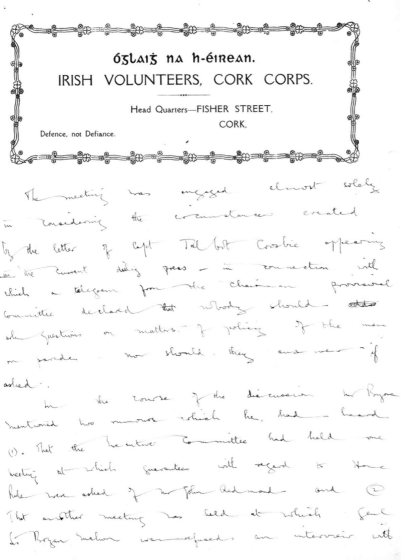

Original minutes of the meeting of the Executive Committee of the Cork Corps of Irish Volunteers held on the night of 29 August 1914
[Courtesy of Cork Public Museum]

That Capt. Talbot Crosbie be and is hereby suspended from membership of this committee, and that this committee demands his removal from the Cork City Command and from the Inspecting Officership of the county corps.[24]

Copies of these resolutions were forwarded to the Provisional Committee and to Colonel Moore. The meeting also reaffirmed its resolution of 5 August and Mac-Curtain was directed to notify the press accordingly.

In a last attempt to influence the rank and file a leaflet – *Volunteers Stand Fast!* – *Capt. Talbot Crosbie versus the Provisional Committee and the Irish Volunteer Organisation* – was hastily printed and circulated. This stated that there was in fact no friction within the unit, 'except the uneasiness caused by Capt. Crosbie in secretly offering the services of the Cork City Corps to the British War Office unconditionally and without the authority of a single member'. It ended by stating that, 'Capt. Crosbie challenges the Cork Volunteers to choose between himself and the Provisional Committee' and asked the Volunteers to choose between 'an ex-English army officer' and a list of thirty-six names of prominent supporters and members of the Volunteers throughout Ireland.[25]

On the morning of Sunday, 30 August, over 1,000 Volunteers made their way to the Cornmarket and arriving at the gate they were met by members of the Executive Committee and handed the leaflet outlining their position. Talbot Crosbie was then approached by Walsh and given MacNeill's telegram and copies of the resolutions passed by the Executive Committee the previous night. At noon Walsh called the Volunteers to attention and formed them into a 'hollow square'. Talbot Crosbie however, insisted on taking up his parade position as commanding officer, and then addressed the Volunteers reiterating all of his previous arguments. Walsh, Fawsitt, MacCurtain, O'Hegarty and Pat Ahern then put forward the position of the Executive Committee, while Thomas Byrne (a Redmondite member of the committee) and H. P. F. Donegan (a solicitor and member of A Company), addressed the gathering, and reminded them that Redmond only envisaged employing the Volunteers in defence of Ireland.

The atmosphere was tense and de Róiste later recalled that: 'there was much excitement, strong language [and] recriminations. At times it looked as if a dangerous situation would arise [as] some of the men were armed with revolvers.'[26] While Walsh recalled 'the seriousness of the situation will be better appreciated when it is recalled that ... discipline, existed only in name.'[27]

After a very full and lengthy debate, matters finally came to a head when Thomas Byrne put the following question to Talbot Crosbie: 'Does Capt. Crosbie want to commit the Cork City Corps to offer their services to fight in any part of the world that Great Britain sends them to, or does he stand by the offer made by Mr John Redmond that you are prepared to defend the shores of Ireland against all comers?'[28] The captain replied, 'I answer emphatically that I will not commit the Cork City Corps beyond what Mr Redmond has committed them to'.[29]

This response was received with loud and prolonged cheering in the ranks, as some broke into song belting out 'for he's a jolly good fellow'. Walsh later recalled that at that stage, 'the Redmondites were ready for anything and whole companies moved towards the platform, brandishing their deadly weapons. The weak elements standing for Sinn Féin on the platform and elsewhere would have been cut to pieces were it not for the intervention of Capt. Crosbie'.[30]

In a further attempt to control the situation, the Executive Committee then asked all those present 'who stood for Ireland' to step forward. The overwhelming majority of the Cork City Corps decided to rally behind their commanding officer and only seventy Volunteers, including all the officers, stood firm in support of the Executive's position.[31]

At this point Talbot Crosbie stepped forward and gave the order to dismiss the

VOLUNTEERS, STAND FAST!

CAPT TALBOT CROSBIE VERSUS THE PROVISIONAL COMMITTEE AND THE IRISH VOLUNTEER ORGANISATION.

The Volunteer organisation has been formed to maintain the rights and liberties of every Irishman on Irish soil.

Captain Crosbie states in yesterday's Press "that it is an open secret that there has been for some time past considerable friction between different sections of the Volunteers."

This statement is an absolute falsehood. There has been no friction except the uneasiness caused by Captain Crosbie in secretly offering the services of the Cork City Corps to the British War Office UNCONDITIONALLY and without the authority of a single member.

This offer was repudiated by the Cork Committee, and Captain Crosbie admitted on parade that he had no authority to make the offer.

Volunteers, do you realise what this offer means?

It means that you Volunteers were offered to the British War Office by Captain Talbot Crosbie to fight under the Union Jack anywhere and for any cause.

In questions of policy the Cork Volunteers have in all cases worked in complete harmony with the Provisional Committee, which since its reorganisation has the confidence of all Irish Nationalists.

Nobody can have any objection to such men as Captain Crosbie or Major Gerald Dease rejoining the British Army; they are entitled to their opinions. But they must not be allowed to misuse the positions conferred on them by the Volunteers by acting as recruiting sergeants for the British Army.

When Home Rule is an accomplished fact, and the Irish people have liberties to defend, the nation can rely that the Cork Volunteers will do their part to support the promise recently made on their behalf by Mr John Redmond, to join with the Ulster Volunteers in defending the shores of Ireland.

Volunteers, stand fast!

We have a precedent for stating that if you agree to Captain Crosbie's proposal, a wire will be immediately sent to the British War Office stating you are now ready to embark for the Continent as part of the British Expeditionary Forces.

Captain Crosbie challenges the Cork Volunteers to choose between himself and the Provisional Committee.

Choose, then!

On one side you have an ex-English army officer. On the other side you have the following :—

Right Rev Monsignor A Ryan, P P, V G
Very Rev Canon Murphy, Macroom
Very Rev J McCafferty, Adm, Letterkenny
Rev F J O'Hare, Newry
W H K Redmond, M P
Joseph Devlin, M P
T J Condon, M P
The Mayor of Sligo
Ml Governey, Chairman Carlow Co C'nc'l
J Creed Meredith, B L, Dublin
John D Nugent, T C, Dublin
J T Donovan, M P, B L, Dublin
J P Gaynor, B L, Finglas
P Murphy, Solr, Waterford
T P Anley, Glasnevin
Joseph Hutchincon, Drumcondra
C J. Kenny, J P, Dublin
S J Hand, Dublin
J J Scannell, J P, Dublin
J F Dalton, J P, Drumcondra
M J Burke, Belfast
J F Small, J P, Clones
Geo Boyle, Derry
Dr Madden, Kiltimagh
Prof Eoin MacNeill, B A, Dublin
The O'Rahilly, Dublin
John Gore, Solr, Dublin
E Martin, Dublin
Sir Roger Casement, C M G
P H Pearse, B L, B A
Bulmer Hobson
J Colbert, Dublin
Sean MacDermott, Dublin
P Beaphy, Dublin
M J Judge, Dublin
J Fitzgibbon, Dublin

Leaflet distributed to members of the Cork Corps at the meeting held in the Cornmarket on Sunday 30 August 1914
[Courtesy of Cork Archives Institute]

parade, after which the Volunteers shouldered him around the parade ground before reforming into companies and marching off through the city streets before formally dispersing outside the headquarters at Fisher's Street. Talbot Crosbie lost no time publicising his victory and immediately penned a letter which appeared in the following morning's *Cork Examiner*:

To
The Editor
Cork Examiner

Sir,

Today a resolution was unanimously adopted by the Cork City Corps endorsing the proposals of Mr John Redmond made in the House of Commons affirming their determination to defend Ireland against foreign aggression.

> M. TALBOT CROSBIE
> Chief Inspecting Officer County Cork
> Irish Volunteers
> Cork 30th August 1914[32]

The same issue also carried a report of the parade in the Cornmarket which was followed some days later by another letter to the editor from MacCurtain setting out the Executive Committee's position:

Sir,

In view of the statement of alleged dissensions in the Irish Volunteers of Cork city the following resolution passed on August 5th was unanimously re-affirmed at yesterday's meeting of the Executive Committee: 'That the committee of the Cork City Corps of Volunteers approves of the proposals set forward by the Provisional Committee Irish National Volunteers and are prepared to act unanimously in accordance with their recommendation namely: That the Irish National Volunteers are prepared to join with the Ulster Volunteers for the defence of Ireland.' The following members were present: Messers J. J. Walsh, T.C., J. F. O'Riordan, T.C., D. O'Mahony, T.C., J. L. Fawsitt, M. Conway, T. Donovan, J. O'Sullivan, P. Corkery, L. de Róiste, P. Harris, H. Lorton, Tom Barry, T. Barry, T. Byrne, J. Jennings, J.P. Lane, M. Bulmer, P. Ahern, S. O'Hegarty.

> T. MacCurtain
> Hon. Sec.[33]

Having read their newspapers the citizens of Cork were left in no doubt as to the deep divisions running through their Volunteer unit. The RIC, who had also been keeping a very close eye on developments, now decided to take advantage of the weakened position of the Executive Committee by moving swiftly against the chairman.

On 8 August the British government introduced an emergency piece of legislation in the House of Commons called the Defence of the Realm Act. Commonly known in Ireland as 'DORA', the legislation was designed to prevent collaboration between Irish republicans and Germany and empowered the government to make emergency regulations for public safety. People breaking these regulations could be tried by court-martial and the Act would prove to be one of the most effective weapons in the 'legal' arsenal employed by the British against the Volunteer movement.

In Cork the most militant members of the Volunteers and IRB were employed by the Post Office. Shortly after the outbreak of the war the military authorities decided to remove these men from locations where they could have access to sensitive information. P. S. O'Hegarty, whose position as postmaster in Queenstown (Cobh) enabled him to monitor the naval base at Haulbowline, was considered to be a serious threat and in early in August he was charged with being 'in recent communication with the German Ambassador.'[34] Under the terms of DORA he was transferred to England on survey work and while not pleased at leaving Cork he nevertheless accepted his posting.[35] However, as events subsequently proved, his removal was only the first step taken by the British authorities against the republican leadership in Cork.

During the Cornmarket parade Walsh had noticed detectives from RIC headquarters at Union Quay monitoring the proceedings. The following morning as he made his way to work at the General Post Office he was stopped by the same officers. They informed him that Dublin Castle had issued an instruction ordering him to leave Ireland immediately but he could take up alternative employment at the Post Office in Bradford, England if he wished. Walsh was shocked: 'in this altogether unexpected dilemma, I sought advice from the few colleagues that I was able to reach in the brief time that remained. They advised me to go and await events. I accepted this advice. Having had time to think it over in my new surroundings, I soon realised that I had made a major mistake; that, in fact, I should have stood my ground come what might.'[36]

Meanwhile the political establishment in Cork continued to support the British war effort and on 2 September William O'Brien and Tim Healy, the two members of parliament for Cork organised a public meeting at City Hall to encourage recruitment for the British army. Dr Dowse (the Protestant bishop of Cork) and Lord Barrymore also spoke. Knowing that some of O'Brien's followers were unhappy with this policy, Fawsitt drew up a pamphlet derisively entitled 'All for England League' which argued against offering the Volunteers for service in the British army. Riobárd Langford, Michael O'Cuill and Donal Óg O'Callaghan tried to distribute the document during the meeting but there was a very hostile reaction from the crowd and they were evicted from the hall.[37] At this point several other Volunteers who had also infiltrated the meeting attempted to disrupt proceedings by scattering cayenne pepper amongst the crowd. However they were also quickly identified and evicted thus enabling the adoption of a resolution assuring the British government that 'The manhood of Ireland was at it's command'. O'Brien himself then concluded matters by declaring that 'Irishmen should say we are ready to fight for England'.[38]

In the meantime a very fragile and tense unity continued to prevail within the Executive Committee and all of the members attended the meeting held on 6 September. This was the first meeting since the Cornmarket parade and when the minutes of the meeting of 29 August were read, Talbot Crosbie asked permission to make a personal statement. He requested that all matters in the minutes be struck from the record as the Home Rule Bill was scheduled to be passed in parliament on the following Wednesday. He argued that if the bill was passed the position of the Volunteers would be radically altered while if it wasn't, the movement would, in effect, become a revolutionary organisation.[39]

At this point it was pointed out to Talbot Crosbie that, the matter having already been referred to Volunteer headquarters, it was now out of the hands of the Executive Committee – and even if they wished to do so, they could not now comply with this request. However, in the interests of fairness, and in order not to prejudice any opinion which might be offered by Colonel Moore, the committee agreed that Talbot Crosbie's suspension from the committee be left in abeyance until the headquarter's decision was made known.[40] It was also decided that no further action would be taken by any member of the committee and that on Saturday 3 October they would reconvene to draft a statement which would then be laid before the Volunteers explaining the differences that had arisen within the committee. If the corps were to divide as a result of this, efforts would be made to ensure that the process would be done as amicably as possible with provision being made to use the same instructors and parade ground and, if the situation so required, they would act together in the interests of their country.

Meeting again two days later on 8 September, the committee received a letter dated 5 September from Colonel Moore notifying them that he had accepted Talbot Crosbie's resignation from his Volunteer positions in both city and county. Then, a letter from Talbot Crosbie was produced denying any such resignation, forcing the committee to vote on the matter. In spite of strong vocal support from some supporters, a majority voted to accept Talbot Crosbie's resignation ordering that this information to be immediately communicated to all units.[41]

This move effectively ended the Volunteer career of Talbot Crosbie and there is no record of him attempting to overturn the decision of the committee. The Battle of the Marne was then raging and the captain probably considered it his patriotic duty to rejoin the British Army. His departure was a significant victory for those committee members who opposed Redmond's ideology. Equally the Redmondite lobby lost its most charismatic leader, while the Corps as a whole lost the most experienced military officer it possessed at that time.

The Executive Committee were now acutely aware of the damage Talbot Crosbie's departure might cause. In an effort to maintain the unit cohesion arrangements were made to have a contingent of Cork city Volunteers participate in a parade of Volunteers from east Cork at the Show Grounds, Midleton, on Sunday, 13 September, to be addressed by Joseph Devlin the Irish Party MP for West Belfast.

Five hundred Volunteers drawn from the companies of the Cork City Corps, led by an officer carrying the national colours, and accompanied by a pipe band, made their way to Midleton and joined approximately 1,400 Volunteers from east Cork under Capt. John F. Walsh, commanding officer of the East Cork District. John Muldoon, the Irish Party MP for east Cork also attended the gathering which saw most Volunteers clad in a 'uniform' consisting of civilian clothing with haversack and bandolier, with a small number equipped with rifles. After the formal inspection Devlin addressed the parade:

> Fellow countrymen, permit me to congratulate you on this splendid demonstration of the manhood of Ireland and of the unchangeable and indestructible spirit of Irish nationality. No country and no cause can ever be defeated so long as it can command the devotion and self – sacrifice of men such as are assembled here today ... In a few weeks – nay, in a few days – after the Irish leader had given the signal, three hundred thousand of the best fighting men in the universe sprang to arms, prepared for any service in the cause of their country which the Irish Party might call them to make.[42]

Having assured the Volunteers that he was confident that the Home Rule Bill would be placed on the statute book within a week, he then went on to say:

> It shows how complete the victory which has been won by the constitutional methods perfected by Davitt and Parnell, which have been so faithful of good to the country until now, and which will carry us, within a few days, to the crowning of their work in the placing of the Home Rule Bill on the Statute Book.[43]

John Muldoon and Capt. Walsh also addressed the parade, expressing similar sentiments and when the speeches were finished the Volunteers sang 'A Nation Once Again' after which they marched from the Show Grounds to the end of the town with Devlin, Muldoon and John F. Walsh at their head.

Devlin's speech disappointed the Executive Committee because it did not speak out against Volunteer participation in the war itself. However Devlin was proved correct in relation to Home Rule and on 18 September the king gave his 'royal assent' enabling the bill to be placed upon the statute books and passed into law. Implementation, however, was suspended until the end of the war.

Aware that tide of public opinion was slowly beginning to turn against the stand taken by the Executive Committee, Terence MacSwiney decided to publish his own weekly paper – *Fianna Fáil (Soldiers of Destiny)*. However, the cost of producing such a journal was beyond his means and to finance publication MacSwiney sold his one prized possession – a collection of books which he had slowly and methodically built up over the years. His sisters tried to dissuade him on the grounds that, because of the war the collection would never realise its true value. 'A bed to lie on, and enough food to keep life in us to enable us to work, is all any of us should think of now,' he replied, and unable to change his mind, his sisters decided to sell their own books as well.[44] The entire collection was eventually sold for £20. This money was used to pay the printer and the first edition of *Fianna Fáil* was published on Saturday, 19 September in which MacSwiney said:

The present crisis has called us into being not to disseminate news, but principles; to help in framing a policy for Ireland, consistent with her sovereign rights, that will seize the opportunity of the moment and restore to her the supreme power of deciding her affairs within and her relations without.[45]

The following day (20 September), John Redmond, in response to the placement of the Home Rule Bill on the statute books, reviewed a small parade of Volunteers at the village of Woodenbridge, in Co Wicklow and told them:

The Empire is engulfed in the most serious war in history. It is a war for the defence of sacred rights and liberties of small nations. Ireland would be false to her history if she did not willingly bear her share in its burdens and sacrifices. This war is undertaken in defence of the highest interests of religion and morality and right. I say to you therefore, your duty is twofold – go on drilling and make yourselves efficient for the work, and then account for yourselves as men not only in Ireland itself, but wherever the firing line extends, in defence of right, of freedom and religion in this war.[46]

Reaction to Redmond's speech by the Provisional Committee in Dublin was swift and a manifesto was promptly issued to the entire Volunteer organisation. Having outlined the history of Redmond's involvement with the Volunteer movement, the document then went on:

Mr Redmond, addressing a body of Irish Volunteers on last Sunday, has now announced for the Irish Volunteers a policy programme fundamentally at variance with their own published aims and objects, but with which his nominees are, of course identified. He has declared it to be the duty of the Irish Volunteers to take foreign service under a Government which is not Irish. He has made this announcement without consulting the Provisional Committee, the Volunteers themselves, or the people of Ireland, to whose service alone they are devoted.

Having thus disregarded the Irish Volunteers and their solemn engagements, Mr Redmond is no longer entitled, through his nominees, to any place in the administration and guidance of the Irish Volunteer Organisation. Those who, by virtue of Mr Redmond's nomination, have heretofore been admitted to act on the Provisional Committee accordingly cease henceforth to belong to that body, and from this date until the holding of an Irish Volunteer convention the Provisional Committee consists of those only whom it comprised before the admission of Mr Redmond's nominees.[47]

First edition of Fianna Fáil
[Courtesy of Cork Public Museum]

The document announced that the Provisional Committee would call a convention for 25 November to re-affirm the original Volunteer Manifesto adopted at the inaugural meeting; to oppose any diminution of Irish self government that had already been placed on the statute books; to repudiate any undertaking made or consent given to legislative dismemberment of Ireland; to declare that Ireland could not, with honour or safety, take part in foreign quarrels other that through the free action of an Irish national government; and to demand that the current system of governing Ireland from Dublin Castle by British military power cease forthwith.[48] It was obvious to Volunteers throughout the country that the movement had reached a crossroads – with members facing a choice between supporting the leader of the largest political party in Ireland, and the man viewed as having successfully negotiated Home Rule or supporting the leadership of the Provisional Committee.

As far as Redmond was concerned the views of the Provisional Committee had become irrelevant. He was the leader of the Irish Party and an elected representative. The Provisional Committee represented a minority view and had become an irritation. It was now time to assume leadership of the entire Volunteer organisation and establish his own national committee.

The battle lines were clearly drawn across the country and in Cork the majority on the Executive Committee had no doubt as to the gravity of the situation. At their next meeting, held on the night of 28 September, Terence MacSwiney proposed that: 'we express our confidence in the Provisional Committee of the Volunteers on their issuing a manifesto condemning Mr John Redmond's actions'.

After heated debate a vote was eventually taken in the early hours of Sunday morning the motion was passed by a vote of sixteen to three. Those who voted in favour were: J. J. Walsh, Maurice Conway, Terence MacSwiney, Patrick Corkery, J. Murphy, Seán Jennings, Patrick Ahern, H. Lorton, Tom Barry, Seán O'Sullivan, Seán O'Cuill, Patrick Harris, Liam de Róiste, J. P. Lane, Diarmuid Fawsitt, and Tomás MacCurtain. The three who voted against were George Crosbie, J. F. O'Riordan and Thomas Byrne.[49] This was the last meeting of the Executive Committee attended by Redmond's nominees and marked the beginning of the 'formal' fragmentation of the Cork Corps.

Determined to seize the imitative the Executive Committee next passed a resolution supporting the Provisional Committee in Dublin and circulated it to all units in a letter issued by MacCurtain:

Terence MacSwiney
[Courtesy of Cork Public Museum]

Irish Volunteer, Cork City Corps,
H.Q. Fisher Street, Cork
October 3, 1914

A Chara,

I am directed to forward to your corps for adoption the following copy of a resolution adopted unanimously, by the Executive Committee, Cork City Battalion, Irish Volunteers.

'That we congratulate the Provisional Committee, Dublin on the determined stand they have taken in keeping the Volunteer movement intact as an army for the defence of the rights and liberties of the Irish people, and we pledge our unstinted support to the founders of the movement in resisting the efforts being made by Messers. Redmond and O'Brien to make the organisation a recruiting ground for the British army.'

Mise. Do chara,
Thomas MacCurtain,
Honorary Secretary[50]

By now Volunteers in both Cork city and county had begun to follow their own conscience with the vast majority opting to side with Redmond. In some units, such as those at Tinker's Cross and Mallow, the entire membership came out in support of Redmond.

The situation within the Cork Corps was replicated all over the country. Unit after unit began dividing on the issue of the war with ultimately the overwhelming majority, with over 170,000 Volunteers, choosing to follow Redmond and taking the name 'Irish National Volunteers'. The minority, initially about 12,000, decided to remain loyal to the Provisional Committee in Dublin. Dominated by personnel who were also members of the IRB, this latter group retained the movement's original title, 'Óglaigh na hÉireann', became known as the 'Irish Volunteers', and set about rebuilding an entire organisation.[51]

4

Reorganisation

As the leadership of the Irish Volunteers in Cork assessed their situation it soon became clear that any re-building process was going to prove extremely difficult. Intense bitterness existed between both Volunteer camps and according to Riobárd Langford (then a second lieutenant with C Company), in the immediate aftermath of the split only twenty-six Volunteers remained with the Executive Committee, the majority of which were officers.[1] However the Executive Committee did manage to retain one important military asset upon which to build a new organisation – the Volunteer headquarters at Fisher Street, complete with arms and equipment.

The National Volunteers were forced to seek an alternative headquarters and the Hibernian Hall was chosen as a suitable storage facility for their limited supply of weapons. However plans were soon underway to acquire further arms and ammunition by raiding Fisher Street. On the night of Thursday, 1 October, while the Irish Volunteers were training in the Cornmarket, a small group of National Volunteers, under the command of Thomas Byrne, forced their way into the building. The caretaker was the only one present, and the raiding party succeeded in removing around 100 rifles together with some instruments belonging to the pipe band. John J. Hogan, then a captain in the National Volunteers later recalled:

> On the evening of 1 October while the extreme section of the Volunteers were drilling at the Cornmarket, a picked team of our men raided the armoury and removed the rifles in motor cars by a circuitous route to the out-offices in my father's stable yard at Clanloughlin where, entirely without my father's knowledge, they remained until we had reformed our ranks.[2]

The Irish Volunteers were outraged by this action, especially since many of the weapons had been purchased individually and several others had been bought from the money collected in Cork for the Defence of Ireland Fund. De Róiste however, later described the raid as 'ludicrous' because many of the stolen rifles were quite old.[3] One Volunteer later described them as, 'weapons used by the soldiers of Garibaldi in the Papal War of the sixties, and [that] their age entitled them to a final resting place in the museum in Fitzgerald's Park'![4]

Then, during a committee meeting held on the night of 3 October the Executive Committee suffered a further setback when Seán Jennings reported that John Donovan, their chief instructor together with another instructor by the name of Long were withdrawing their services.[5] In response, J. P. Lane was unanimously elected the new commanding officer. The committee then reaffirmed their loyalty to Eoin MacNeill and his colleagues and attempted to secure the loyalty of the rural units by passing the following resolution which was circulated to all units by Tomás MacCurtain:

> Irish Volunteer, Cork City Corps,
> H.Q. Fisher Street, Cork
> October 3, 1914
>
> A Chara,
>
> I am directed to forward to your corps for adoption the following copy of a resolution adopted unanimously, by the Executive Committee, Cork city battalion, Irish Volunteers.
>
> 'That we congratulate the Provisional Committee, Dublin on the determined stand they have taken in keeping the Volunteer movement intact as an army for the defence of the rights and liberties of the Irish people, and we pledge our unstinted support to the founders of the movement in resisting the efforts being made by Messers. Redmond and O'Brien to make the organisation a recruiting ground for the British army.'
>
> Mise. Do chara,
> Thomas MacCurtain,
> Honorary Secretary[6]

Unfortunately MacCurtain's letter had little or no impact. When it was received in Clonakilty, the local committee 'ordered it be thrown into the waste paper basket' and the following resolution adopted in its place:[7]

> That we, the members of the Clonakilty (Lord Carbery) Corps of the Irish National Volunteers, in pursuance of notice, strongly condemn the action of the dissenting minority of the Dublin Provisional Committee in seeking to bring about the disruption of the Volunteer movement. That we recognise the authority of the national committee now formed under the presidency of John Redmond, the leader of the Irish Party and we thoroughly endorse his policy.[8]

The use of the Cornmarket was also contentious. The Irish Volunteers quickly made clear their intention to hold their normal Sunday parade there on 4 October. However, the opposition, now under the leadership of George Crosbie, Thomas Byrne and J. F. O'Riordan were also determined to retain control of this facility. They printed a notice under their names in the *Cork Examiner* convening a meeting at the Cornmarket for one o'clock the following day to elect officers and a new committee stating:

> As recent developments in our ranks have been calculated to injure the National Cause, it is imperative that all supporters of a United Ireland should show by their presence that the policy of disruption must cease'.[9]

It was clear that confrontation was inevitable and the leadership of the Irish Volunteers decided that rather than risk a melee they would hold their Sunday parade at Fisher Street instead and a notice to this effect was posted in the evening newspapers.

Accordingly at one o'clock on Sunday, 4 October, hundreds of National Volunteers from Cork city were free to assemble at the Cornmarket where they were joined on parade by a further 150 comrades from the Blackrock Corps. Irish Party members of Cork Corporation and many notables from clerical, civil, legal and commercial establishments in Cork also attended to see the National Volunteers form-up in a 'hollow square' and then acclaim George Crosbie as their new chairman.

Addressing the parade Crosbie admitted that he was doing so in peculiar circumstances. He went on to say that from the outset he desired no quarrel with any section of his fellow countrymen but that those now before him had come together with a definite understanding of what they were about. 'The Volunteers have been brought into existence,' he said, 'in order to train, equip, and arm a Volunteer force for the defence of Ireland and the advancement and preservation of Irish rights and the maintenance of Irish national self-government'.[10] Quoting John Redmond's declaration that 'We will maintain here in Ireland, in fact and inviolable, our Irish Volunteers'. He declared his belief that this meant no man who joined the ranks of the Irish Volunteers would under any circumstances be called upon to fight outside the shores of Ireland. However, if an Irish brigade was formed – separate from the Volunteers –while no man would be asked to join it, if any chose to do so, their wishes would be respected and the Volunteers would wish them well.

Turning to the issue of Home Rule Crosbie stated that 'Ireland has been pledged for two generations before the world that when she got the right of nationhood she would then be prepared to take up her position as one of the members of the British Empire'.[11] While accepting that this had not as yet come to pass he stated his belief that the current political situation represented 'as much of a treaty between two countries as was the treaty made in 1839 that guaranteed Belgian neutrality'.[12] Discussing whether Home Rule might in fact divide Ireland, he said that as far as he was concerned:

> The one way to make division of Ireland certain was to enter upon an anti-enlisting crusade. Everyone wanted to see a United Ireland but the moment the cry against recruiting was raised every unionist in the country would [then] say, 'We have done with you'.
>
> … It was the duty of every Irishman to ratify the treaty made with England, and to take no account of the men who would lead them into a situation which would keep them forever crying 'War, war war' – a policy that was a danger to no one in particular, but which would be a source of disruption and annoyance to our country.[13]

Crosbie's speech was greeted with loud cheers and applause and he was followed by John J. Horgan who proposed the following resolution:

> We, the members of the Cork Corps of the Irish National Volunteers, assembled here on parade; in pursuance of notice, condemn the action of the dissenting minority of the Dublin Provisional Committee seeking to bring about the dissolution of the Volun-

teer movement. We recognise the authority of the national committee now formed under the presidency of John Redmond, the leader of the Irish Party, and we thoroughly endorse his policy.[14]

Turning his attention to Sinn Féin Horgan claimed:

> Small coteries of Sinn Féiners who did nothing to forward the Home Rule cause, and who seemed to have a happy knack of attracting all the cranks in the community, sought to dominate the Volunteer movement, to control its funds and to give no real representation to any other real body of nationalists. This condition of things could not continue and they had come there today to terminate it decisively. The Volunteer movement is a democratic movement and must be controlled by the majority of the Volunteers.[15]

Not surprisingly Horgan's resolution was adopted unanimously and a further one dealing with the issue of command and control was then proposed by H. P. F. Donegan:

> That in consequence of the action of the Cork Executive Committee in siding with the minority of the Provisional Committee in Dublin and declaring their opposition to the policy of Mr Redmond, we declare them unsuitable to hold office, and, as empowered by the resolution of the national committee, we now proceed to elect officers and a committee to control the affairs of the Cork Corps under the direction of the national committee. Before taking office or assuming duty, every officer and member of the committee and each divisional company and sectional commander shall sign a declaration that he recognises the authority of the national committee.[16]

Seconded by J. F. O'Riordan this motion was also carried unanimously. Crosbie then stepped down as chairman and Thomas Byrne took his place.[17] By the time this meeting was over any hope of co-operation or reconciliation between the now rival Volunteer groups had totally disappeared.

While the National Volunteers were conducting their business in the Cornmarket, the Irish Volunteers were parading in Fisher Street where, in spite of everything, over 200 men had reaffirmed their original non-party declaration, and pledged support to the Provisional Committee in Dublin.

However, the overall position of the Irish Volunteers in the city began to deteriorate further when the corporation withdrew permission to use the Cornmarket and the local press ceased to publicise their activities, contemptuously referring to them in reports as the 'Fisher Street Volunteers'. This led to growing hostility from the citizens of Cork which resulted in parades being stoned, Volunteers jeered at, and collection boxes spat upon at church doors and elsewhere. The departure of those who had previously served in the British army also resulted in a dramatic decrease in weapon proficiency and a significant lowering of training standards.

Having successfully dispatched Walsh into exile, the authorities then decided to move against Seán O'Hegarty, the secretary of the Executive Committee and leader of the IRB in Cork. O'Hegarty was employed as a telegraphist in the General Post Office in Cork and in October, the Secretary to the Irish General Post Office, Arthur Hamilton Norway, told him that he was being sent immediately to Derby in England on 'relief work'. This was not compulsory under post office regulations and officials could nominate a substitute if one was available. O'Hegarty promptly sought to have a substitute nominated but his request was refused. He then had an interview with Norway and asked if he was being punished for some offence. Norway informed him that he wasn't being punished but if he refused to leave Ireland he would be dismissed for disobedience.[18] Backed into a corner O'Hegarty was forced to again declare his unwillingness to travel whereupon he was dismissed from his employment.

Having failed to remove him from Cork by transfer to Derby the authorities now decided to serve O'Hegarty with the following order:

> Headquarters,
> Queenstown Fortress
> Queenstown
> October 14, 1914.
> To:
> Mr O'Hegarty
> 1 Wellington Place
> Sunday's Well
> Cork.
>
> In exercise of the powers invested in me by the Defence of the Realm regulations, 1914, you are hereby ordered to leave and remain out of the following areas: The County Borough of Cork; the Urban Districts of Midleton, Queenstown and Youghal; the Rural Districts of Bandon, Cork, Kinsale, Midleton, Youghal No. 1 and No. 2, within twenty-four hours of this order being served on you, having first reported in writing your proposed place of residence to the Fortress Commander, Queenstown.
>
> In the event of your not complying with any of the terms of this order you are liable to be tried by court-martial and sentenced to penal servitude for life or any less sentence.
>
> (Signed) C. Hill
> Fortress Commander
> Queenstown.[19]

O'Hegarty had no choice but to leave the city and eventually went to Gougane Barra where he worked as a labourer. A short while later the post office wrote re-offering the position in Derby but no inducement could shake his determination to remain in Ireland and continue serving the Irish Volunteers.

Walsh however had by now departed for Bradford and Diarmuid Fawsitt had been elected acting chairman in his place. For Fawsitt and his colleagues, the prospect of sustaining existing numbers and then building up a new organisation looked very daunting. However, as Liam Ruiseal later wrote:

> We, the minority group stuck together. From here [Fisher Street] we went on route

marches, through the town, to the outskirts of the city and into the country for mano-euvres. We were looked upon with curiosity and cynicism. The Royal Irish Consta-bulary knew every one of us. Here in Fisher Street we met practically nightly, drilling and receiving instruction. Though small in numbers, most of us had served our appren-ticeship in the language movement, and somehow the language, like a spiritual movement, gripped us, and made us have a deeper and greater love of country.[20]

Drawing up a new 'Manifesto' that October, the Irish Volunteers hoped to explain their case in detail to the citizens of Cork, but the press refused to publish it.[21] Had they done so their readers might have learned why the Executive Committee had acted as they did and what issues had generated the split in the first place:

Despite misrepresentation, vilification and felon-setting in the press of the city, the founders of the Cork Corps, being convinced that the formation of an Irish army was a good thing for our country, a guarantee for the future liberty of Ireland and a safeguard for the rights of Irishmen fought on ...

That which the executive had, in the face of many difficulties and dangers for nine months done everything, short of what they conscientiously believed to be aban-donment of the principles of Irish nationality, to avoid, has now taken place in despite of all their efforts for unity and discipline.

The cause of the division in the Volunteer ranks is not a personal, sectional, or party one. It is one of principle and can be stated round the following questions; 'Has the time come for Irish nationalists to abandon the old principles of Irish nationality to make peace with England; accept the English connection; take a willing place in the British Empire; and, as a consequence, enlist in the British army, and encourage enlist-ment?' Each individual Irishman must answer those questions according to his con-science and his knowledge of what he believes to be right and for the best and highest interest of our nation. The Cork Corps, Irish Volunteers, take their stand by the old tradition. They support the Provisional Committee in Dublin because that committee is true to the original non-party declaration of the Volunteers, and because it refused to allow the Volunteer Organisation to become a recruiting ground for the British Army

To those who agree with us we appeal for moral and material support so as to build up a strong Corps in Cork, which Corps will be at the service of the Irish nation alone and in Ireland. 'For Ireland, in Ireland' is our motto. It has been acknowledged that the Volunteers were a determining factor for good in the Home Rule negotiations. We are confident that, as an independent Irish military force, they will also be a factor for good in the future in helping securing our nation's rights and maintain its liberties. It, therefore, behoves every young Irishman who can join our ranks, and those who can-not join actively to assist in the proper equipment of this Volunteer army of Ireland. The best thanks of the Cork Corps are extended to the citizens of all classes and parties who have already given us such generous assistance.

On the day after the secession, our chairman was, on twenty-four hours notice, re-moved from the city to England; one of our honorary secretaries has since been dis-missed from his employment in the Cork Post Office, and, by order of the military authorities, banished from the city, though his superior officers distinctly state they have no cause of complaint against him. Several others of our officers and men have been threatened with removal or dismissal from employment. We are aware of a secret campaign of terrorism against some of our men, because of their loyalty to Irish nati-onalist principles as hitherto accepted by the Irish people. We feel sure that every honest, honourable and right-minded citizen condemns such unworthy tactics, and will rally to our support in consequence, and help us to defeat this tyranny and co-ercion. Though the press of the city be closed to us – the Press that should be first to strike for fair play and freedom of opinion – we shall take care to inform the citizens of the true facts of all cases of victimisation for principles as occur. And for every man that is struck because he loves Ireland more than England, Russia France, or Belgium, we expect ten men to rush to our standard. GOD SAVE IRELAND.[22]

In Dublin the national leadership of the Irish Volunteers was also pressing ahead with its efforts to rebuild the movement. A special meeting of the remaining mem-bers of the Provisional Committee assembled on 10 October and elected Eoin MacNeill as the new chief-of-staff and approved a new constitution that spelled out the objectives of the organisation:

To secure and maintain the rights and liberties common to all the peoples of Ireland.

To train, discipline, and equip for this purpose an Irish Volunteer Force which will render service to an Irish national Government when such is established.

To unite in the service of Ireland Irishmen of every creed and of every party and class'.[23]

Two weeks later, on Sunday, 25 October, the first convention of the Irish Volun-teers took place at the Abbey Theatre, Dublin, with 160 delegates from all over the country attending – including Tomás MacCurtain representing the Cork Corps. At this meeting it was agreed that a General Council of sixty-two members would govern the movement.[24] Eoin MacNeill was unanimously elected chairman of the General Council and The O'Rahilly elected as treasurer. Provision was also made for a subordinate nine-man Central Executive that would meet on a weekly basis.[25]

One month later, on 25 November, a com-mittee of military organisation was appointed and they drafted proposals for the establish-ment of a new general headquarters. These pro-posals were presented to a special meeting of the Central Executive on Saturday 5 December and forwarded to the General Council at its first meeting the following day where they were approved. The Chief-of-Staff was Eoin Mac-Neill; Director of Arms, The O'Rahilly; Direc-tor of Training, Thomas MacDonagh; Director of Military Organisation, Patrick Pearse; Direc-tor of Military Operations, Joseph Plunkett; and Quartermaster General, Bulmer Hobson. The fact that four of the new headquarters staff were also prominent members of the IRB pro-vided a clear indication of the direction likely

1798 pikehead pattern cap badge worn by the Cork Brigade, Irish Volunteers, from 1915 to 1917
[Courtesy of Capt Tom O'Neill]

to be followed by the organisation.

Soon after, a 'General Scheme of Organisation' was introduced which saw the main Volunteer tactical unit designated as the 'company'. This was then divided into two 'half-companies', each consisting of two 'sections' composed of two eight man 'squads' and a number of specialists. The total company establishment was one hundred and three.

Provision was also made for the formation of Volunteer 'battalions' under the command of a commandant. These would comprise four or more companies but not to exceed eight in total, and plans were made to establish specialist engineer, transport, supply and communications battalions and a hospital corps. Volunteer 'brigades' commanded by a brigadier general would also be formed and consist of three or more battalions but not exceed five in total.

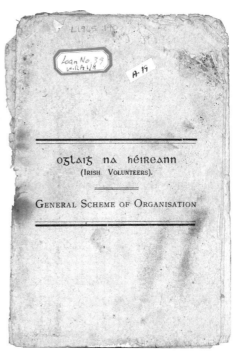

Booklet outlining the Irish Volunteer General Scheme of Organisation
[Courtesy of Cork Public Museum]

This scheme once implemented was designed to place the Irish Volunteers on a sound military footing, a development that would significantly diminish the command function exercised by local committees. During the transition phase provision was made for the formation of temporary 'county boards' consisting of delegates appointed by each company, two nominated by the General Council, and a further three members who would be co-opted. In Cork Tomás MacCurtain presided over the county board for Cork and was also elected to be the Cork city delegate on the General Council, while Terence MacSwiney was elected as the delegate for Cork county.

In the meantime the National Volunteers were actively building on the nationwide support they had received immediately after the split. A new uniform was designed, based on British army pattern, with similar rank markings, but darker green in colour than the original grey green material which was still worn by their rivals. Support from Redmond and the Irish Party enabled them to strengthen their organisation throughout the country and obtain funding to purchase further quantities of weapons and equipment. Then, on Thursday 15 October the organisation's official journal, *The National Volunteer*, made its first appearance priced at 6d.

In Cork the National Volunteers also drew on the support of a youth movement known as 'The Hibernian Boys Brigade' which also trained in the Cornmarket. They received a considerable boost to morale on the weekend of 21 and 22 November when Colonel Maurice Moore, the organisation's commanding officer,

Uniform belt buckle worn by the National Volunteers
[Courtesy of Cork Public Museum]

National Volunteer tunic belonging to Capt. John J. Horgan
[Courtesy of Cork Public Museum]

visited the city accompanied by William Redmond. An inspection took place and new colours were presented to the Cork City Regiment which was now commanded by Lieutenant-Colonel Smith-Sheehan.

Arriving at the Great Southern and Western Railway Station that Saturday night the visitors were met by a guard of honour drawn from B Company of the Cork City Battalion and a huge crowd of nationalists escorted them to the Victoria Hotel. The following morning Volunteers from all over city and county assembled in the Cornmarket where, together with 400 members of the Hibernian Boys Brigade, they formed up behind the Barrack Street No. 1 Brass and Reed Band and at one o'clock marched off to the Mardyke. There, the ceremony commenced at 1.30 p.m. and when the colours were presented to William Redmond by Mrs John J. Horgan, Fr John Russell from the North Cathedral stepped forward and blessed them. Two junior officers, Lt Hill and Lt T. M. McGrath then marched forward to receive the colours before falling-in in front of the regiment as the assembled bands played 'A Nation Once Again'.

After the inspection Moore and Redmond both addressed the parade. Moore told the Volunteers that when he arrived in the city the previous night he had never expected to see the vast crowd that awaited him in the railway station and on the way to the hotel. Redmond congratulated all present on a splendid display and then addressed speculation about their future role:

> Men are not joining the Volunteers out of any threat or menace to the people of Great Britain. They are joining to guard the new liberty of Ireland and the Irish Parliament. No man will be compelled to join any other force outside of the Irish National Volunteers and if the day comes when the honour of Ireland requires her sons to go abroad, I will not beat around the bush. I will say, those of you who are willing to go abroad, follow me and I will go with you.[26]

Colonel Maurice Moore and William Redmond take the salute at the review of Cork City Regiment of the National Volunteers at the Mardyke on Sunday 22 November 1914
[Courtesy of Cork Public Museum]

This parade was an impressive show of strength and presented the National Volunteers in Cork in a very positive light. However, the Irish Volunteers were now, slowly, getting back on their feet and held their own parade that Sunday at Fisher Street. Liam de Róiste recorded these events in his diary on the following Tuesday:

> Sunday was a day of great exertion with me. I was out with the Irish Volunteers on Sunday. We made a good show, some 150 or so of us, all armed with rifles, a cycle corps of about 20, a green flag and an ambulance. We marched about 20 miles having manoeuvres on the way; attacking and defending parties; jumping ditches, moving across ploughed fields; scouting and so on
>
> It may be said that our manoeuvres were also playacting, as I described the [National Volunteer] parade as playacting. They may be called as such, but no man who took part in them could think so. To march 20 miles; to jump hedges and ditches; to run across ploughed fields; to carry your rifle ready – even if unloaded as ours were – to snatch a hasty lunch of a few biscuits and cheese with an apple or two to quench your thirst, to be 'out' facing a north-east wind for the most part, for six hours is rather strenuous 'playacting' that burdens one's muscles and sinews and makes one a better man physically.[27]

On the following Sunday a unique possibility arose to attract public attention by participating in the annual 'Manchester Martyr Demonstration' held in Cork to commemorate the deaths of the three Fenians – William Phillip Allen, Michael Larkin and Michael O'Brien who were hanged at Salford Prison on 23 November 1867.[28] This event always generated a public display of nationalism but de Róiste was confused about the proposed participation of the National Volunteers:

Next Sunday the Martyr's celebration is to be held in Cork city. Redmond's Volunteers are to take part in it ... In honouring the Manchester Martyrs they mean to honour the whole Fenian movement – they honour those men who believed in and worked for an Irish Republic, and in the next breath they will declare themselves loyal to England and the British Empire and howl down as 'factionite' the Fenians of today. These celebrations in honour of the Manchester Martyrs are likely to be kept this year on if anything a larger scale than for many years past. And this at a time when all the political leaders of the Irish people are declaring loyalty to the English connection – the very opposite to what the Fenians stood for. We honour the Fenians, yet thousands of young Irishmen calling themselves nationalists are going out to fight for England and the British Empire. How is this to be explained? I think it arises from a sort of muddled belief that the Fenians were only working for Home Rule – that is for the Irish self government within the British Empire. There is a great deal of haziness on the matter of principle over the Irish public mind.[29]

When the parade assembled after mass at the North Cathedral the Irish Volunteers joined up with the various bands and groups who were taking part in the procession – including the National Volunteers. At one o'clock the procession got under way to City Hall, where a public meeting had been arranged. Having passed Parnell Bridge, the four companies of National Volunteers, the Boy's Brigade and the nationalists bands all left the procession and headed off to their own headquarters. The remaining groups, including the Irish Volunteers, carried on to City Hall and took part in the meeting. A resolution was passed – placing on record the people of Cork's 'undying appreciation and adherence to the principles for which Allen, Larkin and O'Brien were judiciously murdered on a British scaffold' and also pledging themselves to 'support our own language, games and pastimes as being the most effective means of combating 'West Britonism'.[30]

Major John MacBride[31] was then introduced to the crowd and made a speech described by de Róiste as 'rank sedition'.[32] He began by drawing the crowd's attention to the absence of J. J. Walsh and the O'Hegarty brothers declaring that he:

> missed three faces from the meeting that day. Three men who were exiled from Cork, and their native county, and Ireland, because they loved Ireland and would be anxious to avenge Ireland's wrongs.[33]

Then, referring to the Manchester Martyrs, he claimed:

> they were a disciplined body of men and the Volunteers of the present day should also be disciplined, and true, and loyal to one another and their leaders. They should cultivate the manly form of patriotism with which the Manchester Martyrs were imbued, and they should be true to their country and the interests of the country.[34]

Addressing the political situation in Ireland he said:

> British domination should come to an end before Ireland could enjoy the full vigour and strength of nationhood. The people of Ireland would never be satisfied until their country was in the same position and exercised the same right as a free country in any other part of the world.[35]

MacBride clearly identified himself with the Irish Volunteers and significantly raised their profile within the city. If the Mardyke parade had been a triumph for the National Volunteers, then the Manchester Martyr demonstration marked a turning point in the fortunes of the Irish Volunteers.

Major John MacBride
[Courtesy of Cork Public Museum]

Commenting on the procession the *Cork Examiner* remarked:

> The most remarkable feature in this years procession was the attendance of several hundred Irish Volunteers in equipment and for the first time since the memorable 23rd November – when Allen, Larkin and O'Brien gave up their lives at Manchester – did a body of Irish nationalists march in broad daylight in an anniversary procession in Cork carrying military accoutrements and trained as military men. The attendance of four companies of National Volunteers (under the presidency of Mr J. E. Redmond) [with] rifles on their shoulders must serve as a reminder of the difference in the Ireland of today and the Ireland of '67.[36]

However, several differences remained unresolved, one of which revolved around ownership of money collected for the Defence of Ireland Fund which was lodged in the Munster and Leinster Bank. The Cork Regiment of the National Volunteers still required a considerable amount of money to fully equip its men. To alleviate this problem Lord Mayor Henry O'Shea, and other leading members of the Irish Party called a public meeting at City Hall on 3 December to establish an 'equipment fund' for the unit. A circular advertising this meeting was distributed throughout the city and stated that no explanation of the funds already collected for the Defence of Ireland Fund had been forthcoming – clearly implying that misappropriation had taken place.

On the night of Monday 1 December the Executive Committee of the Irish Volunteers met to consider whether they should take any action with regard to the circular and meeting in view of the probable charges that would be made against them. The consensus was not to take any action unless and until any charges were made public and to leave the matter in the hands of the treasurers, Liam de Róiste and Seán Jennings.

Then, on 2 December the *Cork Examiner* exacerbated matters by stating:

> the Irish national army, who acknowledge the Irish Leader, John Redmond, as its president, received no benefit from the collections made in the city in July, and hence it is they [who] appeal to the patriotic spirit and generous sentiments of the people of Cork. The money that will be subscribed tomorrow will not be utilised for any party purpose. On the contrary every penny of it will be utilised for completing the equipment of Cork's Regiment of Irish National Volunteers.[37]

Cash Account and Income and Expenditure Account from 27th November, 1913 to 30th June, 1914, and Balance Sheet, as at 30th June, 1914

Cash Account for the Period from 27th November, 1913, to 30th June, 1914

Receipts		Expenditure	
To: -		By: -	
Affiliation	£133 -16 -10	Instructors -	£101 - 1 - 9
General	273 -10 - 2	Rents, including Drill Halls	105 - 1 - 0
Co. Rifle Fund	153 - 3 - 0	Equipment -	14 -19 - 0
Uniform Fund	7 - 1 - 4	Stores -	7 -17 - 9
Volunteer and Defence of Ireland Funds	1,206 - 0 - 8	On Account of Howth and Kilcool Shipments	101 - 6 - 0
Anonymous	60 - 3 - 6	Printing, Stationery Advertising, etc.	60 - 7 - 7
		Wages -	33 - 2 - 7
		Travelling Expenses	8 -15 - 9
		Postage -	20 - 5 - 5
		Sundry Expenses -	40 - 1 - 8
	£1833 -16- 6	Furniture -	21 - 0 - 0
			£513 -18 - 6
		Balance : -	
		Cash in Bank £1,209 - 11 -3	
		Cash in Hand 40 - 6 -9	
		Cash in Hands of Mr. Kettle 70 - 0 -0	1319 -18 -0
	£1833 -16 - 6		£1833 -16 - 6

Balance sheet compiled by Stapleton and Co. on completion of their audit of the accounts of the Cork City Corps of Irish Volunteers
[Courtesy of Cork Public Museum]

De Róiste and Jennings were outraged by these suggestions and viewed them as an attempt to generate more hostility between the two groups. They decided make public the results of an audit of the finances of the Cork City Corps for the period 21 September 1913 to 25 September 1914 conducted by Stapleton and Company of Trinity Chambers, Cork. Copies of the balance sheet were made and were distributed throughout the city for all to read and a letter was published in the press on 3 December refuting all the charges made in the circular.[38]

Nevertheless the City Hall meeting went ahead and a resolution was passed declaring that the Irish National Volunteers deserved the support and confidence of the people of Ireland and a new equipment fund for the Cork Regiment of National Volunteers was established to which over £100 was subscribed that afternoon.[39] The publicity surrounding this event however had succeeded in igniting a war of words between John J. Horgan and Liam de Róiste and Seán Jennings that would be fought in the pages of the *Cork Examiner* over the next two weeks.

Writing to the paper on 4 December Horgan claimed that he had not at any time received an explanation in relation to the original funds, that an account had not been opened in the Munster and Leinster Bank, that the monies collected for the Defence of Ireland Fund had instead been lodged into an old account in the names of J. J. Walsh and Tomás MacCurtain, and that Walsh had subsequently refused to meet him to discuss the matter. He supported these charges by reproducing a series of letters that passed between himself, MacCurtain and de Róiste between 4 and 10 September.[40]

While the Executive Committee had no desire to pursue the matter any further because, as de Róiste wrote in his diary, 'our cause can stand on its merits and needs no labouring by newspaper controversy, and the wish of the Executive of our Corps is to drop it [as] the times are too serious for this kind of entertainment',[41] he nevertheless felt compelled to respond to Horgan's accusation. In a letter printed in the *Cork Examiner* on 8 December, he said he had informed Horgan on 10 September that he intended to adhere to the resolution passed at the City Hall meeting of 31 July and have both himself and M. J. Nagle appointed to the finance committee but that Horgan had asked him not to proceed with this course of action.[42]

Horgan refused to back down and persisted with his verbal assault:

> Even Mr Roche cannot fool the people all the time. The members of the Finance committee, strange to say, had no control over the funds, and the said funds were not lodged in the bank in their name. Practically the entire sum collected had by 10 September been sent to Dublin or spent. Mr Roche has not yet given us an explanation of the breech of a public trust for which he and his friends, Messers. Walsh, Curtain and Jennings, are guilty. Perhaps he will do so now![43]

Totally frustrated by this public banter, de Róiste felt compelled to fire one last parting shot on the subject and wrote a detailed letter to the press on 11 December:

> Mr John J. Horgan is entertaining in his attempts to fool people into a belief that Messers. Walsh, Curtain, Jennings and myself are guilty of a breech of public trust. As the public can see, our fearful crime of 'omission' when analysed amounts to this – we did not drag Mr Horgan from his office to the Munster and Leinster Bank and there compel him to sign his name in a book as one of the trustees for part of the fund of the Cork Corps, Irish Volunteers. There was nothing whatever to prevent Mr Horgan himself, either alone or with others, going to the bank the day following the public meeting of July 31st and then and there take the necessary steps to have the City Hall resolution carried into effect ... Now he wants to cover his own failure to do what he might have done by trying to gull the public into a belief that others were guilty of an omission for which he himself was as much responsible as any.[44]

Referring to the charge that Volunteer funds had been mis-spent de Róiste again drew attention to the fact that a public auditor's certificate and balance sheet had been produced and published and confirmed that Horgan had indeed received an explanation regarding the money collected for the Defence of Ireland Fund:

> In his latest letter his own words prove the truth of what is said, for unless he [Horgan] had got the explanation to which we referred, he couldn't have known what monies were 'sent to Dublin or spent' by 10 September. The fact of having nothing to hide or be ashamed of we gave Mr Hogan every information he required regarding the monies of the corps. But by a kind of innuendo he now tries to fool people into a belief that there was something wrong. One would imagine from what he has said that the elected executive of the corps, or its Finance Committee, had no right whatever to spend money on behalf of the corps, no power over its own funds, and should not have

touched them before a certain date without Mr Horgan's gracious permission ... The monies of the Defence of Ireland Fund were contributed for the purpose of arms and ammunition for the Cork Corps, Irish Volunteers. They have been used for that purpose and that purpose alone. The National Volunteers, with whom Mr Horgan is now connected have benefited to the extent of at least £100 by that fund. They undoubtedly would have benefited to a greater extent had Mr Horgan agreed to act in accordance with my notice of motion and had not their leaders prematurely forced a 'split'.[45]

De Róiste concluded by saying:

Mr Horgan knows the law. He knows that legally as well as morally every act of the Cork Corps, Irish Volunteers has been right and just, everything square and above board, but by statements unworthy of him he seeks to give a wrong twist to their actions and 'to fool the people all the time.[46]

The matter of the disputed funds ended there with relations between the two competing groups of Volunteers in Cork remaining reasonably cordial. In fact, relations between them never deteriorated to a point where hostilities broke out and this was a tribute to the leadership on both sides. That both groups could peacefully co-exist was evident for all to see when they both participated in the formalities to welcome Douglas Hyde, president of the Gaelic League, to Cork on the night of 15 December to address a public meeting at City Hall.

Hyde arrived at the Great Southern and Western Railway Station around 7.30 p.m. and was welcomed by the lord mayor, the Gaelic League's Ard Coiste Corcaigh, and a representative body of Cork citizens which included Fawsitt, Seán Jennings and de Róiste. After the official welcome, Hyde was escorted to a carriage outside the station. Drawn up in front of him were A and B Companies of the Cork Regiment, National Volunteers under the command of Capt. John J. Horgan and A, B, C, and D Companies of the Cork Corps, Irish Volunteers under command of Seán O'Sullivan, together with contingents from Fianna Éireann and the Boys Brigade.

Hyde was escorted through crowded streets to City Hall were he addressed a public meeting seeking support for the Gaelic League. During his speech Hyde claimed that the Volunteer movement was tapping into funds which would otherwise go to the Gaelic League. However, he wasn't complaining since 'the renewed feelings of social pride and nationhood engendered by the Volunteer movement will in the long run, turn to the benefit of the language movement since nationality divorced from language is an absurd and impossible doctrine'.[47] Commenting on the 'lamentable differences' within the movement, he received sustained cheers and applause when he referred to the escort he had just received. He was pleased the way that both bodies of Volunteers had shaken hands over the Gaelic League and hoped that this would be a precursor to a coming together and a real unity between the Volunteers of that great county and city.

But unity was now just an aspiration. Events were conspiring to drive both camps even further apart as the British authorities in Ireland began to increase the pressure on the Irish Volunteers. The RIC continued to maintain a high level of surveillance on public meetings, while route marches and the personal activities of high profile members were regularly monitored. Then, in early December orders were issued to suppress a number of publications (including MacSwiney's paper *Fianna Fáil*),[48] because the authorities considered them to be seditious and financed by what was referred to as 'German Gold'.[49] The *Irish Volunteer* was also listed for suppression but the authorities were foiled because it quickly appeared in a new format when Eoin MacNeill took over as editor from Larry de Lacey. Surprisingly, no attempt was made to seize the weapons held openly by the Irish Volunteers which led de Róiste to comment that, 'they must have thought the pen was mightier than the sword'.[50]

By this time the National Volunteers were also beginning to experience pressure of a different nature. The overwhelming majority of the Irish people had initially enthusiastically supported Redmond's proposal for the Volunteers to participate in the war and large numbers were convinced it was their duty to enlist in the British army following the lead given by Talbot Crosbie and several others. However, the attitude taken by the British War Office towards the National Volunteers was unhelpful and later described by Lloyd George as 'a series of stupidities that sometimes looked liked malignancy'.[51] Redmond had received a promise from Herbert Asquith, the British prime minister that Irish nationalist recruits would be allowed to maintain their national identity by forming their own corps within the British army. While this concession was immediately granted to Ulster unionists it was initially denied to the nationalists. Then, to make matters worse, Irish Party MPs were poorly treated when they offered their services. Redmond's own son, William, was initially refused a commission. His brother, Willie, was only accepted as an officer when he was able to prove that he had previous commissioned service in the militia and Stephen Gwynn, who was fifty years old at the time, was obliged to enlist as a private.[52]

Over 27,000 National Volunteers enlisted in the British army during the first year of the war. There is no doubt that the attitude of the British War Office combined with the departure of so many officers had an adverse effect on the morale, efficiency and administration of those National Volunteers who remained behind in Ireland.[53] To maintain the cohesion and morale of the Cork Regiment, Capt. Donegan approached the British authorities in the city in December and offered to provide Volunteers for guard duty on the two key bascule railway bridges which crossed the channels of the River Lee and connected the naval base in Bantry Bay with the rest of the national railway system. This offer was accepted and on 1 January 1915 the first guard from the Cork City Regiment of National Volunteers was posted on these two vital installations. John J. Horgan later recalled the euphoria that surrounded the event:

No Irish National force had been entrusted with such duties since the days of Grattan's

First bridge guard mounted by the Cork City Regiment, National Volunteers on 1 January 1915. Seated: Sgt T. Foley, Sgt C. P. Murphy, Colour-Sgt C. Creedon, Capt. H. P. F. Donegan, Lt-Adjt W. T. Daunt, Colour-Sgt J. Long (instructor), C. Curtain. Middle Row: Sgt G. Murphy, P. Keane, P. Donovan, D. Connor, D. Barry, J. O'Keeffe, T. Walsh Back Row: T. Burke, C. O'Brien, J. Coyle, J. Cantillon, D. O'Brien, E. Irwin, E. Dwyer [Courtesy of Cork Public Museum]

Volunteers and I believe we were the only body of National Volunteers who were given an opportunity of doing so. As our men marched to their posts for the first time the watching crowds cheered. Our relations with the local military authorities were excellent and I remember on one occasion when a company of Volunteers under my command were route marching near Cork the guard near Ballincollig cavalry barracks turned out to salute us.[54]

However, not everyone in Cork was happy at this development and in a statement published in the *Cork Free Press* on 6 January William O'Brien described the National Volunteers as 'undisciplined partisans' who were controlled by the heads of a 'secret society'. He also accused the War Office of surrendering to Redmond's demands for their recognition.[55] In response to this attack, Horgan persuaded his father-in-law, Sir Bertram Windle, president of Queens College, Cork, to write to the prime minister on 9 January in support of the National Volunteers. Having dismissed O'Brien's statement as both 'mischievous' and 'misleading' Windle referred to the National Volunteers as 'a fine body of men'. He went on:

nothing would do more harm or act more effectively against the growing sense that Ireland is part of the Empire than to tell them in so many words that they are not trusted even to look after a few bridges in the city in which they live. I do venture to press this point on you with all the power I possess and to express the hope that nothing may be done to discourage, but rather everything possible to encourage a movement fraught, as I am convinced that it is, with so great promise for the improvement of the discipline and order of the young men of the country'.[56]

But his plea fell on deaf ears, and in late January the War Office ordered the military authorities in Cork to cease using the National Volunteers for military duties and the leadership of the Cork City Regiment were informed officially of the decision on 7 February.[57] This was not good news for the National Volunteers. Deployment of armed guards on the two railway bridges had represented a high point in the history of the Cork Regiment, and for the organisation as a whole. While 850 members of the regiment subsequently took part in a grand review of 25,000 National Volunteers in the Phoenix Park on Sunday 4 April, 1915, the organisation had effectively been left devoid of a concrete *raison d'être* by the British government. Denied even the prospect of 'guarding Ireland for the Empire', and with most of its more talented and effective organisers now in the British armed forces, the National Volunteers soon became irrelevant in the Irish political and military context.

For the Irish Volunteers, however, life was becoming better, and having survived the turmoil of the split, they had regrouped and were facing the new year with optimism. Weeknight and Sunday parades continued without interruption and the first major 'exercise' of 1915 was held on Sunday 10 January when a small group of Volunteers went on a route march to Blarney. These weekend excursions were also used to stimulate recruiting and on 17 January another march by eighty armed Volunteers took place to Bottle Hill. Recalling this event Liam de Róiste later wrote:

> It was a very strenuous day for the men of the Corps. There was an improvised 'ambulance'. Many wanted to use the 'ambulance' on the return. There were amusing features on the march. At Whitechurch people coming out of the Church after mass wanted to know where the Volunteers were going. Some wag told them there was a German invasion and everyone had been ordered to go in the direction of Mallow! There were rumours of the possibility of our rifles being seized by the police or military. What Dublin Castle or the British military authorities might do regarding the Volunteers was at all times uncertain.[58]

While training continued at grassroot level the Irish Volunteer leaders in Cork also had to complete the restructuring of their unit according to the new scheme of organisation. A new executive was elected on 2 February: Chairman, Diarmuid Fawsitt; Vice-Chairman, Terence MacSwiney; Honorary Treasurer, Seán Jennings; Assistant Honorary Treasurer, William Shorten; Honorary Secretary, Patrick Ahern; Assistant Honorary Treasurer with responsibility for equipment, Seán Nolan; and a committee of eight others. The temporary 'County Board' that had been governing all of the Volunteer units in Cork county disappeared as did the designation 'Cork Corps'. All formations became part of the 'Cork Brigade' which encompassed all of the county and the Military Council became the 'Brigade Head-

The Brigade Commandant and members of the Cork Brigade photographed at the rear of the offices of the Freeman's Journal *in Dublin in 1915*
Front row: *Tadhg Barry (D Company, Cork City Battalion), Tomás MacCurtain (Brigade Commandant), Pat Higgins (D Company, Cork City Battalion)*
Back row: *Daithí Cotter (D Company, Cork City Battalion), Seán Murphy (Brigade Quartermaster), Donal Barrett (OC A Company, Cork City Battalion), Terence MacSwiney (Vice-Commandant) Pat Trahey (2 i/c A Company, Cork City Battalion)*
[Courtesy of Cork Public Museum]

quarters' with the first brigade officers being Brigade Commandant, Tomás Mac-Curtain; Vice-Commandant, Terence MacSwiney; Adjutant, Daithí Barry; Quartermaster, Seán Murphy; and Staff Officers, Seán Jennings, Seán O'Sullivan and Patrick Ahern.[59] However, there was still some confusion as to where the ultimate authority lay. Fawsitt believed the new brigade headquarters now considered itself the 'supreme body' leaving de Róiste to note in his diary that 'to me it shows that we are not quite settled as to whether we are a military or civil organisation'.[60]

In Tomás MacCurtain, the Volunteers of the Cork Brigade were fortunate to find the right man to work through these problems. Notwithstanding the fact that early in 1915, together with his brother Seán, he had just opened a business at 40 Thomas Davis Street in Blackpool, his biographer, Florence O'Donoghue described his incredible enthusiasm for the Volunteer movement:

> at a time when such a venture might be expected to claim priority for his attention, he continued to devote most of his after business hours and all his Sundays to the growing responsibilities and complex problems of the expanding Volunteer organisation. His immense capacity for work and his genius for the selection of suitable subordinates to whom duties could be delegated, enabled him to maintain a close contact with every

phase of development, and exercise a steady but firm control. It was always a kindly and understanding control, always stoutly maintaining his own high standards of personal and national integrity, always holding aloft the ideals of Volunteer service to draw out what was best in the characters of his followers, but tolerant of their limitations and frailties. His own fine patriotic idealism and practical energy in action was an example and a standard for all.[61]

Another positive development occurred on 4 February when Fawsitt, Jennings, MacCurtain and de Róiste signed an agreement leasing a larger building at Sheares Street for use as a new headquarters. While it didn't contain a large hall, the building did have enough of rooms to allow concurrent activities to take place. While moving from Fisher

Volunteer Hall, Sheares Street, Cork.
[Courtesy of Cork Public Museum]

Street was a priority, training also continued. MacCurtain had his first experience of conducting a 'brigade' exercise on 20 February when, under the watchful eye of Earnest Blythe, the recently appointed Volunteer organiser for Munster, one hundred Volunteers from the city marched to Donoughmore and joined twenty men from the Courtbrack Company for 'large-scale' manoeuvres.

The following Sunday a squad was detailed to take the last few weapons and other equipment to Sheares Street. The did this by 'falling in' on Fisher Street with rifles on their shoulders, and marching through the streets of the city to their new headquarters. De Róiste later recorded:

> it was 'slan beo' to Fisher Street. Hard work had been done there; hard when a redressing of the forces had to be made after the ranks had been broken by the call to fight for England. Our numbers were lessened, but the un-subdued spirit of Irish nationality animated those who remained. There had been great nights in Fisher Street. We stood 'for Ireland only'.[62]

But it was not all good news. The brigade (and the IRB) suffered a serious blow when Seán O'Hegarty was arrested at Enniscorthy, after police raided the home of Larry de Lacy in the early hours of 24 February and discovered a large quantity of arms, ammunition and explosives. O'Hegarty was taken to Arbour Hill Military Detention Barracks in Dublin to await trial by court-martial where, in addition to being charged in connection with the arms and ammunition, the main charge against him was 'distributing seditious literature'.[63]

Throughout this period the Cork Brigade was competing with the British army for new recruits. With thousands of soldiers dying on the western front the British turned to exploiting the heroic deeds of Irishmen within their ranks in an effort to attract new recruits from Ireland. During February the newspapers were full of reports of the bravery of Lance Corporal Michael O'Leary, a native of Inchigeelagh, County Cork and member of the Irish Guards. On 2 February O'Leary had captured a position held by five German soldiers and went on to overrun a machine-gun nest in the vicinity of Neuve Chapelle in Belgium. For this act of gallantry he was awarded the Victoria Cross, becoming the first Irish soldier to be awarded that medal in the war and the first member of the Irish Guards to be so decorated. On 2 March, two meetings were held in the City Hall under the chairmanship of the lord mayor and attended by many leading businessmen. One was held to honour O'Leary while the purpose of the other was to establish a 'recruiting committee' for Cork city and county.

The Cork Brigade also embarked on its own recruitment campaign at the beginning of March. Large numbers of posters were put up throughout the city and county but when the RIC tore them down it was obvious that public demonstrations remained the best method of attracting new personnel. The forthcoming Saint Patrick's Day parade would provide MacCurtain with the first opportunity to put his new brigade in the public eye. To create the best impression possible Capt. J. J. 'Ginger' O'Connell was sent from general headquarters in Dublin to run a course of military training from 8–13 March. He also ran a series of lectures on the status of the war in Europe using official published dispatches and a series of maps. All who attended found O'Connell to be an excellent instructor.[64]

Meanwhile the Cork City Regiment of National Volunteers were busy preparing for the 'Grand Review' scheduled to take place in Dublin on 4 April. To generate support and also encourage enlistment a letter from the adjutant, W. T. Daunt, was published in all local newspapers on 27 March in which he identified sixty-four officers and men from the regiment, headed by Captain Maurice Talbot Crosbie who had enlisted in the British armed forces.[65] However within days the *Cork Constitution* began to treat the figure of enlistments with contempt – 'sixty-four out of a thousand?' it queried. Daunt countered stating that the National Volunteers in Cork had 'never numbered more than 500, of whom only 300 were effective'. Presented with an opening the *Cork Constitution* decided to exploit it and expressed astonishment at the figures suggesting previous claims that 'thousands' of Redmondite Volunteers existed in Cork were wildly incorrect, and that national figures were probably wrong as well.[66]

The Irish Volunteers remained aloof from this debate concentrating instead on the Saint Patrick's Day parade being organised by the Ard Choiste of the Gaelic League. On the evening before-hand the Cork City Battalion was inspected by Eoin MacNeill in the Volunteer Hall and on the following day MacCurtain proudly led 300 Volunteers through the streets of Cork accompanied by their own pipe band.[67] Most wore some item of military equipment, a small number were dressed in full uniform, the majority carried rifles, and thirty rural Volunteers were armed with 'croppy pikes', similar to those carried by the United Irishmen in 1798.

Not everyone was impressed with this show of force and at the beginning of May the brigade again became the focus of attention from the authorities, with J. J. Walsh once more the prime target. Dismissed from the post office in Bradford, because it was discovered that he had written to Cork Corporation protesting against a proposal to confer the freedom of the city on Lord Wimbourne, Walsh had written to Fawsitt to tell him that he was coming home. However, when his train arrived at Mallow Station on 6 May, he was met by Capt. Wallace Dickie, a British army intelligence officer, and a detective from Union Quay RIC Barracks. They handed him a letter which, under the terms of the Defence of the Realm Act, outlined where he was not permitted to reside within the whole country and Walsh was ordered to return to Dublin or face immediate arrest. Having little option he chose to return to the capital on the next train where within a short time he would play his own unique part in course of Irish history.

The Volunteers had assembled in Cork at the Great Southern and Western Railway Station to welcome Walsh home, and when they learned what had happened at Mallow they marched back to Sheares Street in an angry mood accompanied by a large crowd. An impromptu public protest meeting took place in the street outside, and addressing the crowd Fawsitt drew their attention to a recent newspaper headline which read 'Huns off the Cork Coast'. This referred the sinking of a ship by German submarines off the Old Head of Kinsale but in light of what had just happened to Walsh, Fawsitt said that far from being off the coast, 'The Huns are at our gates'.[68]

Having made their protest, the Cork Volunteers had to carry on without Walsh. Anxious to build on the success of the Saint Patrick's Day parade it was decided to hold a fund-raising concert in the Opera House on 9 May. This drew a large crowd and proved to be a great success.

While these events were unfolding in Cork Seán O'Hegarty appeared before Mr Justice Kenny and a Grand Jury at Green Street Courthouse, Dublin between 7–11 April. He was found not guilty on a range of charges related to the discovery of arms and explosives at de Lacy's house. However, the jury could not agree on a verdict in relation to the 'seditious literature' charge so the trial was adjourned and O'Hegarty was remanded in custody. A further blow was struck against the brigade leadership when, on the night of 21 May, a detective sergeant from Togher RIC Barracks delivered a letter to Fawsitt on behalf of Brigadier-General Hill, ordering him to leave Cork county within five days. The Executive Committee immediately held a meeting to discuss what course of action they should take if other members were served with similar notices, but as no direction on the matter had been received from headquarters a decision was deferred until a later date.

In response to this development George Crosbie, president of the Cork Industrial Development Association convened a meeting at which he suggested that Fawsitt, who was still Secretary, should immediately go to the United States as a representative of the association. Faced with the alternative, which would involve immediate incarceration if he remained in Cork, Fawsitt reluctantly chose to go abroad.[69]

In the midst of all this MacCurtain was trying to remain focused on military matters and on 23 May he led a contingent of around 300 personnel drawn from Cork city, Blarney, Mallow and Charleville to take part in a parade in Limerick city. Together with units from Limerick, Dublin, Clare, Kerry and Tipperary, the Cork Volunteers assembled under command of Capt. Robert Monteith and then marched proudly through the city streets before passing the Treaty Stone in review order. De Róiste was there to see the spectacle:

> it was a thrilling sight to see those marching men, rifles on their shoulders, heads erect, keeping time to martial music. Thrilling to know this body of Volunteers stood 'for Ireland only'. Blandishments, propaganda, intimidation, coercion, had failed to subdue them.[70]

Not everyone was delighted to see them and the *Cork Examiner* reported what occurred as the parade passed through the Irishtown district of the city:

> a number of residents, principally women and youngsters, many of whose relatives are in the army gave a very distinct display of dissent. Hissing and booing was indulged in, and a number of missiles, chiefly cabbage stumps, potatoes, and pieces of dried mud, as well as some stones, were thrown.[71]

Later that evening when units converged on Limerick railway station for the journey home the Volunteers found another hostile crowd waiting for them composed for the most part of 'separation allowance women'. Once again an assortment of missiles was thrown in their direction but this time many units decided to defend themselves with their fists and some personnel fixed bayonets and adopted defensive stances. The Cork contingent were amongst the last to arrive at the station. They too were met with hostility but their officers wasted little time ordering 'fix bayonets'. This action had the desired effect and enabled them to force their way into the station to board the train although stones and bricks continued to rain down on top of them.[72] At the end of the day the Cork contingent returned home unscathed, and as de Róiste noted, 'they even managed to bring back two rifles more than they had taken with them'.[73] They also received a morale boost a week later on 7 June, when thanks to a brilliant defence mounted on his behalf by T. M. Healy, Seán O'Hegarty was acquitted of the remaining charges brought against him. Although not permitted to set foot in Cork city he was allowed to return to Ballingeary where he immediately resumed his Volunteer and IRB activities.

However with Fawsitt in exile, the Executive Committee were still faced with electing a new chairman and when they eventually convened on the morning of 12 June Terence MacSwiney was duly elected. After long discussion a decision was also taken binding all military and civilian officers to remain in Ireland in the event of deportation orders being served on them.[74]

Development and expansion of rural units remained a priority at this time because, following the split, only 300 Volunteers from companies based in Bantry, Ballingeary, Ballinhassig, Cobh, Courtbrack, Castletownroche, Gurteen, Tinker's Cross, Kilpatrick, Kinsale, Mallow, Mitchelstown, Tracton and Tullylease remained loyal to the Executive Committee.[75] From the beginning of 1915 MacCurtain and other staff officers including MacSwiney, Daithí Barry, Pat Higgins, Seán Murphy, Seán Nolan and Pat Trahey, usually accompanied by a piper, would leave Cork every Sunday for some rural destination to improve standards in training and administration. They then stood on platforms outside church gates after Sunday mass urging the men of the area to join the Volunteers.

Efforts to attract new recruits also continued within the city. Ordering his

Ógláiġ na hÉireann.

(IRISH VOLUNTEERS.)

——o——

CORK CORPS.

——o——

MEMBER'S CARD.

——o——

Name *Caoimhġealbaic Mac Suibġe*

Address *4 C..... ....*

Rank ....

Company ....

Number ....35...............

Irish Volunteer membership card belonging to Terence MacSwiney
[Courtesy of Cork Public Museum]

companies to parade on 29 July to commemorate the successful Howth landings the previous year MacCurtain reminded his men:

> membership of the Irish Volunteers carries with it grave responsibilities; responsibilities greater than any other organisation demands. Now is the time for our men to show whether or not they can be relied on to stand true to their signed pledge on the declaration form; now is the time to take your place in the ranks and face aggression from whatever quarter it may come; now is the time to show whether you have the courage of your convictions. Our men are being struck at; your plain duty is to stand by them; and by your presence show that you are prepared to uphold the tradition established at Howth on 25 July 1914.[76]

After the parade he addressed a public meeting outside headquarters at Sheares Street and invited all young men in the crowd to join the ranks of the Irish Volunteers, inspiring some to enlist on the spot.

Two days later MacCurtain led a contingent of 100 Cork Volunteers to Dublin for the public funeral of the great Fenian leader, Jeremiah O'Donovan Rossa.[77] While civic dignitaries representing all shades of nationalist opinion attended the ceremonies, the funeral turned into a major show of strength for the Volunteer movement. Contingents gathered from all over the country watched by immense crowds lining the streets. The Volunteers escorted O'Donovan Rossa's remains to Glasnevin Cemetery and so great was their numbers that those from Cork were unable to gain entry and never heard Patrick Pearse render his famous oration:

Tomás MacCurtain leading the contingent of Volunteers from the Cork Corps who travelled to Dublin for the funeral of O'Donovan Rossa
[Courtesy of Cork Public Museum]

the defenders of this realm have worked well in secret and in the open. They think they have pacified Ireland ... They think they have foreseen everything; but the fools, the fools, the fools – they have left us our Fenian dead; and while Ireland holds these graves, Ireland un-free shall never be at peace.[78]

De Róiste marched in the ranks of the Cork Volunteers and left this account of events:

> Rossa's funeral demonstration was almost beyond description. It was stupendous, over-whelming, extraordinary, significant in view of the times and circumstances ... *The Irish Times* computed that 7,000 men, at least, 'of military age' carried rifles in the procession. There may have been ten or twelve thousand Volunteers in all marching; Óglaigh, National Volunteers and Citizen army men. I estimated that there may have been 200,000 spectators. No British soldiers, no police were to be seen. Dublin that day was controlled by Irish Volunteers.[79]

Upon returning home the Cork Brigade still had pressing local matters to deal with. One of these revolved around the fact that both de Róiste and MacSwiney were at that time employed by The Cork Committee of Technical Instruction and in July that body decided to reduce its staff. Notice of dismissal was issued to de Róiste but when MacSwiney heard of it he immediately tendered his resignation, on the grounds that he was the junior man, thus enabling de Róiste to be reinstated. This move turned out to be a blessing for the Cork Brigade because the following month MacSwiney was appointed full-time Volunteer organiser for County Cork. As his biographer, Moirin Chavasse explained, MacSwiney was an inspired choice for this task:

> It is true that MacSwiney was an excellent and tireless organiser, well educated and well read, able to speak and write effectively, but the real source of his influence lay in his personal qualities – his power to inspire heart and mind with his own idealism, his

unassuming nobility of character, his sincerity. Perhaps what chiefly distinguished him was that most difficult and costly of things, self-mastery, carried to an heroic degree, in the ever deepening surrender of his life to the Will of God, and the indefinable influence over others that always accompanies this.[80]

Accompanied by other brigade officers MacSwiney spent his weekends travelling the county by either train or bicycle addressing crowds coming from mass, or lecturing at meetings of the Gaelic League and GAA on the aims and objectives of the Volunteer movement. He was so successful establishing new companies that P. S. O'Hegarty later wrote: 'in that capacity he was wonderful. All over Cork he went on his bicycle and the living flame sprang up behind him'.[81]

However, training within the existing units of the brigade also remained a high priority and during the summer of 1915 the quest for excellence was pursued relentlessly. Liam de Róiste was among those Volunteers who were put through their paces and on 21 August he wrote this account of an exercise he took part in:

> One of the finest nights of my life was spent last night, a night operation with the Óglaigh boys. It was a glorious moonlit night up in Gurranabraher, at the top of a high hill overlooking the city we were. There were attacking and defending forces, I was with the latter. The actual place to be defended was a place called 'The Croppie's Grave'. We lay as sentries in the grass by the side of a 'ditch' each man at an interval of some yards. Silence reigned supreme at times and I looked at the bright moon, slightly brown in the haze and at the stars. What thoughts at such times. Alas the attack never came off. There was some misunderstanding as to the actual spot and the attacking forces did not discover us before the time arranged for discontinuing the operation but it was all well and useful and pleasant as we marched back 'at the double' – good indeed it was!'[82]

Two day later a small group of Volunteers from the city battalion was dispatched to Millstreet where Patrick Pearse was giving an oration at an Aeriocht and they were to escort him back to the city to address a group of Volunteers at Sheares Street on 24 August. Liam Ruiseal was one of that escort party and later recalled:

> We were accompanied by two Cork Volunteer pipers. We went by train to Macroom and then by waggonette to Millstreet. On the return journey, as we reached a rise of ground near Carriganimma, all got down except for Pearse and myself. We spoke in Irish only, and I remember that he was under the impression that he had met me before. The following night, Monday, he addressed a big gathering in the Hall in Sheares Street. There was great fire in his speech, and he was tremendously inspiring.[83]

While Pearse may have inspired those Volunteers who turned out in full equipment to meet their director of operations, there were also those in the community who wanted nothing to do with him or what he stood for. As Liam de Róiste recorded in his diary, a number of these people made their feelings known that night:

> There was some disturbances caused by soldier's dependents – drunken women who had received their separation allowance on Monday. The disturbance was after the meeting, very vile language was used along with cheers for King George and questions

Headquarters Staff, the Cork Brigade Irish Volunteers on manoeuvres in the summer of 1915 (front row from left to right: Terence MacSwiney, Tomás MacCurtain, Seán Murphy)
[Courtesy of Cork Public Museum]

Irish Volunteer dinner parade at Coosan Camp, Athlone, September 1915 showing Cork Volunteers Donal Barrett (fifth from left) *and Terence MacSwiney* (sixth from left)
[Courtesy of Cork Public Museum]

like, 'why don't ye go and fight for England?' The police left when the disturbance began. Some soldiers apparently were neighbours. Our boys as usual took no particular notice – or took the affair good humourously – the only way'.[84]

GHQ in Dublin was also actively engaged in strengthening the movement nation-wide and that summer a number of officer training camps were organised The first was held in Wicklow in August and the Cork Brigade was represented by Daithí Barry, Pat Higgins, Diarmuid and Michael Lynch and Seán Nolan. Tadgh Barry, Walter Furlong and Seán Scanlan attended a second camp held in the Galtee Mountains that month, and Donal Barrett and MacSwiney were the brigade's representatives at the Athlone camp in September.

On 13 October a new dress instruction was approved and published in the *Irish Volunteer* ten days later:

> Uniform is not compulsory for Irish Volunteers but it is desirable, especially in the case of officers.
>
> Uniform will consist of tunic, breeches, puttees, and cap, of the approved design, in the approved green heather tweed, with dark green shoulder straps and cuffs (leggings may be substituted for puttees at option.)

1915 pattern Irish Volunteer peaked cap
[Courtesy of Cork Public Museum]

> All buttons will be dark green compressed leather. (Volunteers who have already brass buttons may have such buttons oxidised dark green in lieu of getting regulation buttons.) Shiny buttons, marks of rank, cap-peaks and other shiny objects are not to be worn.
>
> A system of ranks and insignia based on stripes for non-commissioned officers and shamrock clusters, or 'trefoils,' and 'wheeled crosses' similar to the design adopted by the Confederation of Kilkenny were approved for commissioned officers:

Rank	Insignia	Position
Squad commander	One dark green stripe	Left breast of tunic
Section commander	Two dark green stripes	Left breast of tunic
Company adjutant	Three dark green stripes	Left breast of tunic
Second lieutenant	One trefoil and one dark green band	Cuffs
First lieutenant	Two trefoils and one dark green band	Cuffs
Captain	Three trefoils and two dark green bands	Cuffs
Vice-commandant	One wheeled cross and three dark green bands	Cuffs
Commandant	Two wheeled crosses and three dark green bands	Cuffs
Vice-commandant general	Two wheeled crosses and four dark green bands.	Cuffs
Commandant general	Three wheeled crosses and four dark green bands	Cuffs

In Cork, meanwhile, as MacCurtain and his staff focused on administration, logistics and training, MacSwiney continued organising the brigade. On 4 September de Róiste noted:

> Terence MacSwiney is organising the county – congenial work for him I should think. There is a strong corps out in Ballinadee near Bandon, and that district is, I believe, going well. Also out in Mallow District things are going well. It is now as easy to get corps started as in the early days of Volunteering, but it is not so easy to keep them going. In some districts the police are very active in endeavouring to intimidate the young men from joining while in other places the priests are opposed. The Redmond Volunteers are defunct in I believe, nearly all the country districts in Co. Cork where they were in existence about a year ago. They exist [now] only in name and only put up a show of activity by ads in the *Evening Echo*. I have often expressed the opinion that I would not wish to see them fall through all together [because] they commit the Irish Parliamentary Party to some form of 'physical force' for the attainment of some form of Ireland's rights. But the merciless illogic of their[current] position must be apparent to [even] many of themselves.[85]

MacSwiney made frequent use of local sporting events, fair days, holidays, and often enlisted the assistance of well known republicans in his efforts to attract new recruits to the movement. In October 1915, for example, he approached T. J. Murray, from Lissarda, Crookstown for help in starting a new company of Volunteers in his parish of Kilmurray:

> the people were divided in politics and apathetic. There was, however, a coming contest in a game of bowls, played among the bye-roads of the parish, sure to draw a large crowd of young people. MacSwiney and a few friends were invited, and made the acquaintance of the local men. Soon after a meeting was called, and a contingent from the Cork Brigade together with the pipe band arrived, accompanied by MacSwiney, MacCurtain, Liam de Róiste and others. They explained the object of the Volunteer movement and of the meeting, and afterwards a drill parade was held by the Cork Volunteers. Recruits were then called for and enrolled and given their first instruction.[86]

Con Meaney remembers MacSwiney's visit to Millstreet two weeks later:

> 1 November 1915, was a Fair Day in Millstreet. It was also a Church Holiday. Arrangements were made for a parade of the small group of Volunteers and for a public meeting. Cork Brigade headquarters sent Terence MacSwiney, who addressed the parade

and the members of the public asking for recruits for the Irish Volunteers. Mr Jeremiah O'Riordan, Corner House, a veteran of the Land League and an old Fenian presided. As a result of the meeting three companies were formed immediately – Millstreet, Rathduane and Mushera. Keale company was formed about a week later.[87]

However, forming companies was one thing, but sustaining them was another and MacSwiney discovered that a considerable amount of time had to be spent encouraging and assisting these fledgling units. While the city companies were relatively well armed, had well trained instructors and the facilities of the Volunteer Hall at their disposal, most rural units had to 'soldier on' relying on the ingenuity of their officers to acquire suitable training aids and equipment.

Con Meaney, a member of the original Millstreet company which had dissolved after the Redmond split, was elected captain of the Mushera company formed on 1 November and the difficulties he encountered were typical at that time:

> There were seven in the company at the first meeting, and by December, 1915, the strength had increased to fifteen ... Parades were held once a week. There were no exservicemen in the company. The training was carried on by me from what I had acquired in the original Volunteer company and from the Fianna Handbook. The training consisted mainly of close and open drill, arms drill with dummies, and marching.[88]

MacCurtain was also aware of these difficulties and, whenever possible, instructors from the city were sent to visit the rural units. But the shortage of arms and ammunition was a constant source of concern and the Volunteers in the Cork Brigade became efficient in a wide variety of military skills – with the exception of marksmanship.

Nevertheless MacSwiney's efforts had proved so successful that by mid November sufficient new companies had been formed to enable MacCurtain and his staff to group them together into 'battalion' formations. The four city companies had already been formed into the 1st Battalion under the command of Seán O'Sullivan. Now the companies located at Bandon, Ballinadee, Clogough and Kilbrittain (together with sections from Ballinaspittle and Kinsale) were formed into the 2nd Battalion commanded by Tom Hales. Patrick P. Twomey of Kilmona took over the command of the 3rd Battalion formed from companies at Courtbrack, Donoughmore, Kilmona, Mourne Abbey and Whitechurch. The 4th Battalion was drawn from companies at Ballinagree, Carriganimma, Clondrohid, Kilmurray, Kilnamartyra and Macroom and commanded by Daniel Corkery. And the 5th Battalion was formed bringing together the companies at Keale, Millstreet, Mushera and Rathduane and Cornelius J. Meaney of Millstreet was appointed commanding officer.

While real progress was being made the Volunteers found themselves under increased surveillance by British military intelligence and as a precaution, Seán O'Sullivan, commanding officer of the Cork City Battalion, increased the security on the Volunteer Hall by posting a full time guard on the premises. Liam Ruiseal was one of the first Volunteers to perform this duty:

In off-duty time, we slept on a bed of straw on the top floor' he later recalled. 'It was a weird experience, pacing the long hall up and down, in the dead of the night, and not a sound to be heard except the footsteps of a policeman on patrol duty outside.[89]

Ruiseal later recalled how he found himself with another mission that November while attending the 1915 All Ireland Hurling Final in Dublin:

As my companion and myself stood on what was later to be called 'Hill 16', we saw Cork lose to Laois. But we had other business besides the match. We called to Fleming's Hotel, a rendezvous, and got a consignment of revolvers for Cork. We were told to separate at Kingsbridge. Everything went well and we brought the arms safely back'.[90]

Due to ongoing organisational development, and the acute shortage of arms and equipment, MacCurtain had only managed to run company-level tactical exercises throughout the year. However the 1915 Manchester Martyr demonstration again provided him with an opportunity to muster his whole brigade. Taking place on Sunday 28 November, the format for the Irish Volunteers was the same as the previous year – nine o'clock mass at the North Cathedral followed by a procession and public meeting at the national monument on the Grand Parade.

The remaining National Volunteers in Cork decided not to attend the 'official' ceremonies and instead attended the 12 o'clock mass at the North Cathedral. Before marching to the cathedral they assembled at the Cornmarket where they were addressed by the newly promoted Lt Col Donegan who told them that they were in the unique position of having been 'invited' to take part in an event which it was their right to control. He said it wouldn't be dignified to participate under those circumstances and after mass they marched back to the Cornmarket where they joined the Queenstown Company and set off into the countryside on a route march.[91]

The Irish Volunteers seized the opportunity and occupied centre stage that day. At 8.15 a.m. they paraded at Sheares Street and marched to the cathedral for the anniversary mass where they joined a number of civic dignitaries, the organising committee and a large congregation. When the procession began forming up on Great George's Street around noon the hard work carried out by MacSwiney and his comrades became very evident as over 1,200 Volunteers from eighteen districts formed up.[92] While only a few were dressed in full Volunteer uniform, and only a small number carried rifles, the majority wore Volunteer caps, belts, bandoliers, haversacks and puttees and were armed with shotguns or pikes.

At one o'clock the procession moved off and, preceded by a number of bands, MacCurtain led his Volunteers along the quays and down Patrick Street where the bands played the 'Dead March' as they approached the national monument. There, under the chairmanship of W. O'Shea, a public meeting began with Seán MacDermott, a leading member of the IRB and a member of the Volunteer General Council, as the main speaker.[93] Paying tribute to the Volunteers he described them as 'men who knew their own minds and understood the cause that brought them together.

*Officers of Cork Brigade together with Seán MacDermott and Herbert Moore Pim
photographed on the day of the 1915 Manchester Martyr's Commemoration*
Back: *Dick Murphy, Seán Nolan, Daithí Cotter, Seán Scanlan, Fred Murray*
Centre: *Tom O'Sullivan & Diarmuid O'Shea* (with rifles), *Tom Barry, Pat Corkery,
Donal Barrett, Donal Óg O'Callaghan, Tadg Barry, Diarmuid Lynch, Con Twomey*
(with rifle)
Front: *Seán Murphy, Tomás MacCurtain, Seán MacDermott, Herbert Moore Pim,
Seán O'Sullivan, Seán Ó Murthile*
[Courtesy of Cork Public Museum]

Men who were strong in the justice of their cause and who were determined to serve that cause'. He concluded by declaring that what made the demonstration appropriate for the Manchester Martyrs remembrance day was the fact that 'it was heard in the tramp of marching feet'.[94]

The Manchester Martyr demonstration proved that the Cork Brigade of the Irish Volunteers, poorly armed though they were, were now a force to be reckoned with. Out of the turmoil that existed at the start of the year, MacCurtain and Mac-Swiney, assisted by the membership of the Executive Committee and Military Council, had built a brigade that encompassed most of the county and now had forty-six active companies in training. However, as the Volunteers made their way home that afternoon in November, they didn't realise that MacDermott and his colleagues in the IRB leadership had already a plan in place for an armed rebellion against the crown.

5

Rebellion

On 2 January, Terence MacSwiney addressed a public meeting at Ballynoe village, accompanied by Thomas Kent, a Volunteer officer from Castlelyons, County Cork. The proceedings were closely observed by the RIC and while MacSwiney was speaking someone in the crowd shouted, 'What will we fight with, our hands?'

MacSwiney, who was wearing full Volunteer uniform, paused, reached into his bandolier, pulled out a bullet, and held it up saying 'Where that came from, more will come.'[1]

On 8 January *The Irish Volunteer* paid tribute to the progress the brigade was making and published a notice advertising that an officer's training school would soon take place at Sheares Street:

> Owing to the rapid growth of the movement in Cork City and County, and the inability of the City Battalion to supply instructors to all the county corps, the Cork Battalion Council have devised a scheme of training, whereby they will be able to place a trained officer over every Corps in the county.
>
> During the past three months, up to thirty instructors were sent out every Sunday to different parts of the county. These men had in some cases to cycle twenty and twenty-five miles before reaching their destination.
>
> So efficient is the work of these men that now almost 70 Corps exist, and still appeals for help are coming weekly to start new ones. At that rate of progress the City Battalion expect that, before January of the new year closes, they will account for at least one hundred corps.
>
> Commandant O'Connell, of Headquarters Staff, has been secured to conduct the school, so that nothing will be left undone to make the course a complete success.[2]

Before the course could take place, the brigade suffered a serious set-back when MacSwiney and Thomas Kent were arrested on 12 January, charged with having made a seditious speech at Ballynoe, and incarcerated in Cork Gaol. Despite this, O'Connell still travelled to Cork and commenced the course as planned on 22 January. Lasting two weeks, and based on an American army syllabus of training it proved a great success. Thirty-seven officers representing almost every company in the brigade attended and were then able to pass on what they learned to Volunteers in their own units.

At this time an atmosphere of tension and expectation began to permeate the ranks of the Cork Brigade and many believed that some sort of armed military action could well be in the offing if the British authorities attempted to forcibly disarm the Volunteers, or introduce conscription. However few if any were contemplating armed rebellion against the crown although in early January James Connolly, the leader of the Irish Citizen Army, delivered a lecture to thirty Cork Volunteers at An Grianán on the military tactics to be employed in such circumstances.[3]

Officers Training Camp at Volunteers Hall, Sheares Street, Cork January 1916
Front Row seated: *Cornelius J. Meaney, Cornelius Mahoney, Patrick J. Twomey,*
Martin O'Keefe, Michael Leahy, William Kelliher, James Murphy, Chris McSweeney.
Second Row: *Seán O'Sullivan, Christopher O'Gorman, Michael Lynch, Seán Lynch,*
John Manning, Charles Wall, James Walsh, Seán Carroll, Riobárd Langford,
Maurice Ahern, Tom Hales, Tadgh Barry, Captain J. J. 'Ginger' O'Connell
Back Row: *Paud O'Donoghue, Cornelius Ahern, Seán O'Driscoll, Eugene Walsh,*
Denis O'Brien, Seán Collins, Seamus Courtney, Jeremiah Mullane, Michael Hyde,
Liam O'Brien, Michael McCarthy
[Courtesy of Cork Public Museum]

However, the majority of the Volunteer movement had no inkling that plans for the establishment of an independent Irish Republic by force of arms were already at an advanced stage. Immediately after the outbreak of the First World War the Supreme Council of the IRB, subscribing to the old Fenian axiom that 'England's difficulty was Ireland's opportunity', decided that an armed rebellion would be mounted in Ireland before the end of the war. This decision was copper-fastened in May 1915 when, with the British army locked in the stalemate of the western front, an IRB Military Committee, comprising Patrick Pearse, Joseph Plunkett and Eamon Ceannt, was formed to draft a plan for an armed rebellion.[4]

The plan ultimately adopted envisaged the mobilisation on Easter Sunday 1916 of over 10,000 Volunteers, supported by Connolly's Irish Citizen's Army. In Dublin the General Post Office and other strategic buildings would be seized, and a series of outposts would be established in the suburbs from which roads and railway lines into the city would be controlled thereby preventing the arrival of British military reinforcements. Volunteer units based in the country would also mobilise, establish a line along the River Shannon and then advance on Dublin capturing or destroying all RIC barracks along the way. However, everything was contingent on the successful landing of a shipment German arms on the coast of County Kerry.

Pearse decided that the Cork, Clare, Kerry, Limerick and Galway brigades would occupy selected positions on Easter Sunday to cover the landing of these weapons. Their positions were within a day's march of their respective headquarters and each unit would receive their quota of arms. The Cork Brigade was selected to occupy positions running along a north-south line from Newmarket to the Boggeragh Mountains and then westward to the Cork-Kerry border where they would connect with units of the Kerry Brigade extending eastwards from Tralee. The Limerick Brigade would maintain contact with the northern end of the Cork position and extend northwards to the River Shannon, while the Clare and Galway Brigades would hold the line of the Shannon to Athlone.[5]

To ensure secrecy, the remainder of the Volunteer leadership and the brigade commanders upon whom the success of the rebellion would depend were not invited to take part in the planning process. From a military point of view this was a serious mistake that was compounded by the fact that plan depended on the successful landing of the German arms. It would also appear that no alternative course of action had been considered. Despite all the military posturing engaged in by the Military Committee, the basic staff work required to generate a realistic objective, develop a concept of operations, and produce at least two viable courses of action in accordance with standard military procedure, was not done – leaving the plan fatally flawed.

MacCurtain was completely unaware of what was in store for his men, but the atmosphere of tension and anticipation remained palpable. The Cork Brigade continued to concentrate on routine training and morale received a boost when Mac-Swiney returned to active duty after he was released on bail on 16 February, although he was subsequently fined one shilling for his 'crime' at Ballynoe. Ever conscious of the ongoing need for publicity, in early March MacCurtain tasked his subordinate commanders to prepare for the annual Saint Patrick's Day parade.

In the meantime the RIC were increasing their operations against the leadership of the Cork Brigade and in the early hours of 15 March, the homes of Mac-Curtain, Seán Jennings and Liam Shorten were raided. While a revolver and some 'incriminating' documentation was found at the home of Jennings nothing else of significance was discovered. The *Cork Constitution* however decided to use the incident to generate friction between the Irish and National Volunteer movements. Referring to the raids the paper claimed that 'acting, we understand, from a hint, if not direct information from the Nationalist Volunteers ... the authorities have at last taken steps to cope with the Sinn Féin Volunteer menace'.[6] The same article also raised the possibility of violence between the two groups at the forthcoming Saint Patrick's Day parade and suggested that feelings between them were running 'very high' arguing that their armed presence should be viewed 'with a certain amount of disquietude, if not alarm'.[7]

Both commanding officers responded by issuing immediate denunciations of the article. MacCurtain said that he had no doubt the *Cork Constitution* was 'using every means in its despicable power to disrupt the demonstration ... for its own jealous party purpose' and was trying to 'destroy the harmony that existed between all bodies in Cork as represented on the demonstration committee.'[8] He had already issued an operational order to the company commanders involved in the

*Operation Order issued
by Tomás MacCurtain
for the 1916 St Patrick's
Day parade*
[Courtesy of Cork Public
Museum]

ꜰɪᴀɴɴᴀ ꜰᴀ́ɪʟ.

Irish Volunteers—Cork Brigade.

St. Patrick's Day Demonstration in Cork City, 1916.

A Chara,

    Your Company is to parade at full strength, and with full equipment, and one day's rations, at above parade in Cork City.

The Brigade will be inspected by an officer of the Headquarters Staff, and special attention will be paid to the condition of arms.

For train arrangements, enquire of the local stationmaster.

Companies will be met on arrival by officers of the Brigade Staff.

Officers will please note the following Orders, which must be strictly adhered to :—

(1) Any breach of discipline must be severely dealt with and not let pass unnoticed.

(2) **On no account** will any man leave ranks without permission from his officer.

(3) Any man using ammunition **without an order**, either before, during, or subsequent to this parade, is to be immediately deprived of his arms, suspended from the organisation, and case reported to Brigade Council for investigation.

    Noᴛᴇ.--The special attention of all ranks is called to above order.

(4) On arrival at Cork all officers will take orders from officers of the Brigade Staff, who will wear a Blue Band round cap.

(5) Any man under the influence of drink will be considered incapable, deprived of his arms and equipment, and forthwith suspended from the organisation, pending trial by courtmartial.

(6) Every Volunteer is responsible for the honour of the Brigade, and should bear himself accordingly.

By Order of Brigade Council,

T. MAC CURTAIN,
Commandant.

parade informing them that no Volunteer would be permitted to 'leave the ranks with permission from his officer', that 'any breach of discipline would be severely dealt with' and that 'any man using ammunition without an order, before, during or subsequent to the parade would be immediately deprived of his arms and suspended from the organisation'.[9]

    Replying on behalf of the National Volunteers, Lt Col H. P. F. Donegan said that the statements contained in the article were 'absolutely untrue, and have apparently been made for the express purpose of stirring up bad blood on St. Patrick's Day.'[10] Not surprisingly, and given that everyone was now on their best behaviour, the parade passed off peacefully with Volunteer contingents from twenty-four different companies of the Cork Brigade participating.[11] The remaining members of the Cork City Regiment of the National Volunteers also took part in the parade. Included at the centre of their formation a was a blank space roped off by eight boys carrying a sign which read 'This space is reserved for four hundred of our com-

The Cork Brigade, Irish Volunteers marching in the 1916 Cork City St Patrick's Day parade
[Courtesy of Cork Public Museum]

rades now fighting for Ireland in the trenches'. If accurate, this was a considerable improvement on the figure of sixty-four which Adjutant Daunt had been claiming the previous year.

Meanwhile, the Military Committee of the IRB were pressing ahead with their own preparations for the rebellion which still remained known to only a select few within the Volunteer movement. It wasn't until early April that MacCurtain was issued orders about the proposed landing of arms in Kerry. He was not informed of the Military Committee's main objective and this accounts for the fact that when Pearse issued a 'General Order for the Easter Sunday Manoeuvres' on 3 April, as far as MacCurtain was concerned his task was only to provide security for the arms' landing.[12]

It was in this context that MacCurtain directed his staff officers to draft plans for an 'exercise' on Easter Sunday that would ensure maximum mobilisation and the deployment of all the available arms and ammunition within the brigade. Funds were also issued to the battalion commanders so they could augment their existing stocks by purchasing rifles, shotguns, explosives and ammunition from whatever source possible. Then, at a tense unit commander's conference at Sheares Street on Sunday, 9 April, MacCurtain informed his battalion and company officers of their respective tasks and the initial points to which each company would march on Easter Sunday, though not their final destination.

MacCurtain also believed there was a real possibility that crown forces might attempt to intercept them and stressed the importance of carrying out their orders. He also said that it was imperative that every weapon, every round of ammunition, and every bit of equipment should be brought out and that all Volunteers should parade with overcoats, blankets and two days rations. Aware of the risks involved, most of the officers of the Cork Brigade left the meeting believing that before long they might be going into action.[13]

Then, on Wednesday 19 April what became known as the 'Castle Document' was circulated. Purporting to have been drafted by the British authorities in Dublin Castle, it outlined detailed instructions for the suppression of the entire Volunteer movement, and was received with outrage by even moderate Volunteers like Eoin MacNeill. In reality Joseph Plunkett and Seán MacDermott had forged the document to incite the Volunteer movement to support the IRB rebellion and initially it achieved its objective. Following a meeting of the Volunteer Executive Council that day MacNeill sent the following order to MacCurtain:

> 2 Dawson Street,
> Dublin
> April 19, 1916

A plan on the part of the Government for the suppression and disarming of the Irish Volunteers has become known. The date of putting it into operation depends only on Government orders to be given.

In the event of definite information not reaching you from headquarters, you will be on the look out for any attempt to put this plan into operation. Should you be satisfied that such action is imminent you will be prepared with defensive measures. Your object will be preserve the arms and the organisation of the Irish Volunteers, and the measures taken by you will be directed to that purpose.

In general you will arrange that your men defend themselves and each other in small groups, so placed that they may best be able to hold out.

Each group must be supplied with sufficient supplies of food or be certain of access to such supplies.

This order is to be passed on to your subordinate officers and to officers of neighbouring commands.

(Signed) Eoin MacNeill
Chief of Staff[14]

Original agenda for the Cork Brigade unit commanders conference held on 9 April 1916
[Courtesy of Cork Public Museum]

Ironically, this order arrived in Cork on Holy Thursday, the day that the Military Committee's plan was beginning to unravel. Bulmer Hobson and J. J. O'Connell had overheard a conversation and they learned for the first time of the IRB's intentions to commence rebellion on Easter Sunday and they immediately reported this to MacNeill.

Furious at having been deceived, MacNeill went to confront Pearse and Mac-Dermott who admitted the truth leaving MacNeill to declare that he would do everything in his power to stop the rebellion. In the early hours of Friday MacNeill drafted the following order:

April 21, 1916

Commandant O'Connell will go to Cork by the first available train today. He will instruct Commandant MacCurtain, or in his absence will select an officer, to accompany him to Kerry. Commandant O'Connell will immediately take chief command of the Irish Volunteers, and will be in complete control over all Volunteers in Munster. Any orders issued by Commandant Pearse, or any person heretofore are hereby cancelled or recalled, and only the orders issued by Commandant O'Connell and under his authority will have force. Commandant O'Connell will have full powers to appoint officers of any rank, to supersede officers of any rank, and to delegate his own authority or any part of it to any person in respect of the Irish Volunteers in Munster.

(Signed)   Eoin MacNeill
                  Chief of Staff

P.S. – Officers in Munster will report to Commandant O'Connell as required by him on the subject of any special orders they have received and any arrangements made or to be made by them as a consequence.

Chief of Staff.[15]

MacNeill also issued a general order to all Volunteer units re-affirming his instructions issued in the wake of the 'Castle Document' to act only on the defensive in the event of an attack or an attempted disarmament by crown forces and was adamant that this order would:

take the place of any orders that may have been issued in a different sense. All orders of a special character issued by Commandant Pearse, or by any other person heretofore, with regard to military movements of a definite kind, are hereby recalled or cancelled, and in future all special orders will be issued by me or by my successor as Chief of Staff.[16]

Later that morning, as O'Connell was on his way to Cork both Pearse and Mac-Dermott visited MacNeill at his home at Woodtown Park. They told him that the German arms shipment had already left Lubeck for Ireland (9 April) on board a captured British auxiliary cruise ship disguised as the Norwegian vessel *Aud* commanded by Capt. Karl Spindler. Given this new information MacNeill was persuaded that it was too late to stop the rebellion, and after much debate he was prevailed upon to countermand his previous order. Once this had been achieved MacDermott ordered Dr Jim Ryan to travel immediately to Cork to inform the Cork Brigade that the rebellion would proceed as originally planned. But the damage was already done. Uncertainty

The Aud
[Courtesy of Cork Public Museum]

Sir Roger Casement on board the German submarine U19
[Courtesy of Cork Public Museum]

now reigned, and in the days ahead this led to total confusion.

MacCurtain had received word from Dublin that O'Connell was heading south and that he should meet him at Mallow Station. Arriving at Mallow he discovered that O'Connell's train had already gone on to Cork. Returning to the city he discovered that O'Connell had gone to Mac-Swiney's home at Grand View Terrace, Victoria Road and when, together with Seán O'Sullivan, he eventually caught up with them he received MacNeill's orders placing O'Connell in command. MacCurtain then issued his own orders cancelling the planned acquisition of a number of motorcars that were to be used in the transportation of the German arms.

Oblivious to events unfolding on land, the *Aud* continued to steam towards Ireland accompanied by Sir Roger Casement in the German submarine *U19*. Casement had travelled to Germany in October 1914 and tried unsuccessfully to raise an Irish brigade from captured Irish prisoners of war. Disappointed at a general absence of German support for Ireland's cause, and the fact that they were only prepared to supply 20,000 rifles, he decided to return home and hopefully persuade the Military Committee to postpone the rebellion. A Volunteer officer, Capt. Robert Monteith and Sgt Daniel Bailey from the ill-fated Irish Brigade, accompanied Casement on board the *U19*. When they disembarked from the submarine and came ashore at Banna Strand, Monteith and Bailey set off for Tralee. Casement was feeling too ill to make the six-mile journey and he took shelter in an old ring fort overlooking the beach at nearby Currahane.

Soon afterwards Bailey was arrested near Abbeydorney but Monteith, managed to avoid capture and made his way to Limerick where he was harboured by the Jesuits. Casement, however, had been observed in his hiding place, arrested by the RIC, and sent to Dublin. Then, in a move that effectively neutralised the Volunteer leadership in Kerry, the RIC arrested two of its senior officers, Austin Stack and Con Collins and imprisoned them in Spike Island.

The *Aud* also met with misfortune. Initially it had been ordered to rendezvous with *U19* off Fenit on Thursday 20 April but this was later changed to Sunday 23 April. Unfortunately the ship was not equipped with wireless and, unaware of the change in plan, remained visible off the Kerry coast for over twenty-four hours before eventually attracting the attention of the British patrol vessel, *HMS Bluebell*. Spindler was ordered by the *Bluebell* to go to the British naval base at Queenstown (Cobh). Rather than allow his ship and cargo to be captured, he scuttled it within sight of Cork harbour on Easter Saturday, and he and his crew were captured and interned for the remainder of the war.

Meanwhile Lt Fred Murray of D Company, Cork City Battalion, was delivering MacCurtain's orders to both the Eyeries and Kenmare companies of the Kerry Brigade, unaware that they had been rescinded. Returning home by train late on Good Friday evening he heard that both Casement and the *Aud* had been captured and upon arrival in Cork in the early hours of Saturday morning he raced to the Volunteer Hall to bring MacCurtain up to date. Horrified at the potential for disaster that was now unfolding MacCurtain instructed Murray to keep the matter to himself for the moment. He told MacSwiney what he had heard, and then set off to meet O'Connell at the Windsor Hotel on King's Street. The situation became further confused when Dr Jim Ryan arrived by train from Dublin with MacDermott's dispatch leaving MacCurtain to respond in frustration, 'tell Seán we'll blaze away as long as the stuff lasts'.[17] But it was never going to be as simple as that – too many conflicting orders had been given, too many rumours were in circulation, and too many critical aspects of the plan were now in disarray.

When news of Casement's capture, and the sinking of the *Aud*, eventually reached MacNeill on Easter Saturday evening he decided that any rebellion launched at this time, in the midst of such confusion and without adequate armaments, was doomed to fail and he immediately issued the following order:

April 22, 1916

Volunteers completely deceived. All orders for special action are hereby cancelled and on no account will action be taken.

(Signed) Eoin MacNeill
Chief-of-Staff

Later that day he issued a more specific order, copies of which were dispatched to units throughout the country and placed in the following morning's *Sunday Independent:*

Owing to the very critical position, all orders given to the Irish Volunteers for tomorrow, Easter Sunday, are hereby rescinded, and no parades, marches or other movements of Irish Volunteers, will take place. Each individual Volunteer will obey this order strictly in every particular.[18]

In Cork however, MacCurtain was acting on the last order he had received from Ryan and throughout Saturday Volunteers of the Cork Brigade prepared for action. All available arms, ammunition and supplies were taken to the Volunteer Hall at Sheares Street, which was also placed under armed guard. Similar activity was taking place at other points throughout the county while rank and file Volunteers availed of an opportunity to attend confession and spend time with their friends and families. The first unit to mobilise was the Cobh Company under the command of Capt. Michael Leahy:

On Easter Saturday afternoon fifteen of us marched to Cork from Cobh, and went to the Volunteer Hall in Sheares Street. Our arms were five rifles and a number of revolvers. The Guard of Cork city men in the hall were allowed to go home, and the Cobh men took over. That night some of us were engaged until the early hours of the morning in bringing cans of petrol and other stores from somewhere in the city to the Hall. There was a driver with us [and] on one occasion we were stopped by the police, and I had to threaten to use my revolver before we were permitted to pass. All of the men were advised to go to confession and did so.[19]

The Cobh Company were later joined by twenty-seven men from the Dungourney Company under the command of Capt. Maurice Ahern who had arrived in the city by train at 8.30 p.m. These Volunteers joined their comrades in last minute preparations for the following day's events and, together with MacCurtain and MacSwiney, they spent the night camped on the floor of the hall trying to snatch a few hours sleep on the beds of straw provided by the brigade quartermaster. Others manned sentry posts and among those detailed for this duty was Seamus Fitzgerald from Cobh who later recalled:

from 2 a.m. to 4 a.m. I was on patrol outside Sheares Street with a loaded shotgun and personal orders from Tomás MacCurtain to shoot any crown forces or others who attempted to interfere with the coming and going of any men running supplies to the headquarters.[20]

Then, as dawn broke on Easter Sunday Volunteers from all over Cork county arose, had breakfast, and armed themselves with whatever weapons they had in their possession. They then said farewell to their loved ones, met with comrades, and set out to their designated assembly points without having any clear knowledge of what exactly was going to happen. The four Cork city companies began to gather at the Volunteer Hall, where Lieutenant Riobárd Langford, of C Company recorded:

MacCurtain distributed first aid outfits – this was the first time they had been issued. Every available rifle was [also] secured. Five rifles, which were held by the O'Sheas in Dominick Street, were not brought to Sheares Street when the men assembled. They were sent for and the parade did not move off until they arrived.[21]

Speculation was rife among the Volunteers about the precise objective of the 'exercise' upon which they were now about to embark. When Dan Donovan of C Company saw the first-aid kits being distributed, followed in close order by tins of Oxo cubes, he turned to a comrade and remarked, 'this looks like the real thing'.[22] Eventually all the relevant supplies were issued and just before noon, the assembled Cork Volunteers 'fell in' outside their headquarters and marched off to the railway station at Capwell where they boarded a train for Crookstown. Unfortunately they had no sooner departed than Jim Ryan arrived at the Volunteer Hall by car and delivered a copy of MacNeill's latest countermanding order to MacCurtain. This placed the brigade commander in an impossible position. All over the county his men were marching to their designated areas, in many cases observed by members of the RIC. He realised that there was no way to relay this new order to all of his subordinate officers in time for them to stand down. He was also acutely aware of his order to resist all attempts by crown forces to interfere with their movements and that any isolated military action in the absence of a general uprising was guaranteed to fail. The situation was fraught with danger and he decided that the only course of action was to permit his men to proceed to their original forming up points before issuing any new orders.

In Dublin the IRB Military Committee was meeting at Liberty Hall that morning to discuss how best to respond to MacNeill's countermanding order. Notwithstanding the loss of the German rifles and the confusion caused by MacNeill's order, they decided to commence the rebellion at noon on Easter Monday. Messengers were dispatched all over the country with new orders even though, in view of the distances involved, it was probable that many units would not receive them in time. The fact that this eventuality bothered none of those now lining up to lead the rebellion was an indication of their commitment and the individual and cumulative sacrifice they were prepared to make.

Meanwhile in Cork MacCurtain and MacSwiney were left wondering how to respond to MacNeill's latest order, given that a total of 1,029 Volunteers, representing seventy per cent of the brigade's strength had now assembled at eight different places: 80 near Lauragh on the road to Kenmare; 29 at Kealkill; 55 at Inchigeelagh; 399 at Macroom; 120 at Carriganimma; 67 at Millstreet; 222 at Bweeing; and 57 at Barley Hill.[23]

Eventually MacCurtain concluded that he had no option but to stand down his men and allow them to return home. As heavy rain began to fall all over the county he ordered David O'Callaghan to drive the one borrowed car at his disposal and accompanied by MacSwiney and Bob Hales he set off for Crookstown. From there he sent the Brigade Communications Officer, Pat Higgins, to find Seán O'Sullivan with orders to dismiss the column marching for Macroom upon arrival at its destination. MacCurtain then went to Inchigeelagh and dismissed those gathered there before moving on to Bweeing where he met T.J. Golden, company commander of the Courtbrack Company who later recalled:

> Tomás MacCurtain appeared to be in a great hurry. He addressed the whole parade and said that the exercises were cancelled. The men were to return quietly to their homes and keep their arms safely. They may soon be wanted again, he said, and may be called upon in the near future. We were to remain alert and 'stand to arms' until further orders.[24]

At the remaining assembly points the officers in charge had been previously been told to stand down their men that evening if no further instructions were forthcoming. When nothing more was heard this order was complied with and the Volunteers of the Cork Brigade set off for home that Easter Sunday night confused and dismayed. They were also soaked to the skin with green dye from their Volunteer hats running down their faces, and marching through the mud, no one really understood why such a major mobilisation had taken place in the first place.

Totally dispirited and frustrated with this chaotic situation, MacCurtain decided to go to Ballingeary to confer with Seán O'Hegarty but the headlights in the car failed, forcing the group to spend that Sunday night at Carrigadrohid. At first light on Easter Monday morning they moved on to Ballingeary and spent the day discussing the latest developments with O'Hegarty. After 8 p.m. they set out for Cork unaware that an uprising was already under way in Dublin.

However, the brigade officers left behind in the city the heard news from Dublin and when it was confirmed that the rebellion had commenced the Brigade Quartermaster, Seán Murphy, and the Officer Commanding Cork City, Seán O'Sullivan, immediately decided to increase security at the Volunteer Hall. They also posted scouts outside the military and RIC barracks and near the city bridges to report any major movement of crown forces and dispatched a cyclist on the one o'clock train to Macroom to find their commanding officer. Both MacCurtain and MacSwiney had already left for Cork and at the outskirts of the city they met Volunteer Denis Breen who briefed them on the developments in Dublin. Shocked and bewildered they went to Sheares Street as quickly as possible and on entering the building they were given a given message from Pearse which had been brought to Cork that day by Mary Perolz, a member of the Dublin Cumann na mBan. Written on the flyleaf of a small pocket diary the message was simple. It read 'We start at noon on Monday' and was signed 'P.H.P.'

Seán Murphy later recalled that this latest communiqué served only to increase pressure on the brigade commander because:

> as the message from Pearse was not a military order it only increased the confusion in Cork [and] all the more so by reason of the fact that it was only initialled, whereas all previous dispatches were fully signed.[25]

Astonished by this latest development MacCurtain was now acutely aware of the heavy responsibility on his shoulders. But his men had just returned home from a gruelling day, and without the arms shipment he knew that even on a good day they wouldn't be in a position to make a stand against an enemy who would now be on full alert. Other than Pearse's message he hadn't received any further orders from MacNeill nor had he received any intelligence reports to indicate what exactly was taking place in Dublin. The situation deteriorated further when unconfirmed reports began to filter through that the British army had deployed artillery on the high ground overlooking the city. MacCurtain later left this impression of the chaotic situation that existed within his headquarters that Monday night:

> Reports were coming in continuously about the fighting which was going on in Dublin since mid-day. Most of the reports were merely rumours, and the boys were in a state of frenzy. We were waiting for some definite information to come to us, so that we could understand what was going on and decide what we should do. Reports were coming in about soldiers going hither and thither in their thousands. Everyone had his own story,

and no two stories were the same. Most of the boys were sensible and steadfast and placed their trust in Terence and me. They were relying on us to do the sensible thing.[26]

That night he knew he no longer had room to manoeuvre. The element of surprise had been lost, his brigade had dispersed, a hostile crowd had gathered outside his headquarters, and in all probability the British army in Victoria Barracks were preparing to move against him. In the absence of any clear orders or information from Dublin, MacCurtain decided not to confuse his men any further and to concentrate instead on defending his own headquarters against attack:

> We had decided not to leave the hall, come what might. We were convinced that the soldiers would surround us and that we would die there, but we were satisfied – no one could say that we had run away from the fight, and indeed there was no such thought in our minds.[27]

According to Riobárd Langford, not all Cork Volunteers were happy with the decisions taken by the brigade staff. He recalled that within the hall that Easter Monday night:

> the situation was very tense and strained. The younger officers particularly wanted to fight, and were resentful of the waiting policy adopted by the leaders. They expressed their views, but the weight of the influence and authority of the older men (as they regarded the brigade officers) was against them. A lead from them would have taken the majority of the Cork men to the fight in some way. Action in the city may have been inadvisable, but there was nothing to prevent the Volunteers mobilising the city on Monday or Tuesday.[28]

One former member of the Cork Brigade was by now in the middle of the action although his former colleagues had no knowledge of his exploits. J. J. Walsh, having been denied the possibility of returning to Cork the previous May, had moved instead to Dublin and opened a small tobacco shop in Blessington Street. He also joined the Dublin branch of the Ancient Order of Hibernians (American Alliance) at North Fredrick Street which had a membership of thirty, some of whom were also Volunteers. When he heard that fighting had broken out on Easter Monday, Walsh immediately put on his Volunteer uniform, slung his rifle, and made his way towards Fairview where he joined a unit of Volunteers commanded by Oscar Traynor. Ordered to disperse and reassemble two hours later Walsh recalled:

Lt Riobárd Langford
[Courtesy of Eoin Langford]

> I plodded my way back to Blessington St with my rifle on my shoulder. On that long trail I met neither policeman or soldier. The people looked scared or bewildered, and no wonder, for rumours of all kinds were flying about. After cooking some food and thinking things over, the idea struck me to mobilise my colleagues of the Hibernian Organisation. I got in touch with Mr Scollan, the Secretary, and within a couple of hours we had rounded up twenty of

its thirty members. At six o'clock, Scollan and myself handed our little company over to James Connolly, at the GPO. From this time forward we were known as the Hibernian Rifles. The next morning news had come that already two of that little band had lost their lives in the defence of the City Hall. During the week we lost a fourth of effectives killed and a number wounded also.[29]

While Walsh settled down to spend Monday night in the GPO, efforts were already underway to prevent an outbreak of hostilities in Cork. When the lord mayor, T. C. Butterfield, and George Crosbie heard of the rebellion in Dublin they contacted Brigadier-General W. F. H. Stafford, the general officer commanding (GOC) in Cork. They suggested that before any attempt might be made to capture the Volunteer Hall by force of arms they should be given an opportunity to persuade the Volunteers to hand over their weapons peacefully and thus avoid any casualties or damage to the city. Stafford agreed and ordered Capt. Wallace Dickie, his ADC and intelligence officer, to take charge of negotiations. Later that evening Butterfield called upon the assistant bishop of Cork, Dr Daniel Coholan, and together they went to the Volunteer Hall at 11 p.m. to ascertain the intentions of the Volunteer leadership. MacCurtain later left this account of the meeting:

> When the two came in the place was in disorder, but we welcomed them and straightened it out as well as we could. They said there were rumours around the town that we were going to rise out that night and they came that they might have the truth. We said there was no truth in the story but that if interfered with we would do our best to defend ourselves. They were satisfied with that and left.[30]

The following morning the fighting intensified in Dublin but all remained quiet in Cork, with individual Volunteers taking the opportunity to make confession, attend mass and receive communion. By now news of the rebellion had spread throughout the county where some company commanders managed to mobilise whatever men ever they could locate but in the absence of any concrete information they too decided to remain in their respective locations and await further orders.

One Volunteer however was unable to wait any longer for something to happen in Cork and decided to make his way to where fighting was taking place. Michael O'Cuill of B Company approached MacCurtain to tell him that he was leaving. While the brigade commander advised against this, he added that that each individual Volunteer had the right to do whatever he considered best. That evening O'Cuill armed himself with a revolver and set off by train for Tipperary where it was reported fighting was in progress. When he discovered that all was quiet he returned to Limerick junction and on Friday morning boarded a train for Dublin only to find his journey terminated at Sallins. He made the rest of the journey on foot and succeeded in getting as far as the northern suburbs of Dublin early on Saturday morning where he was finally captured by a curfew patrol and imprisoned in Richmond Barracks. Having actually played no part in the rebellion, O'Cuill entered Cork republican folklore as 'The man who walked to Dublin'.

Meanwhile efforts to prevent an outbreak of fighting in Cork continued even though, according to Seán Murphy, the British army had by mid-week deployed one field-gun on the hill of Gurranabraher and positioned two or three machine-guns in the Malt House directly opposite the Volunteer Hall.[31]

On Wednesday, MacCurtain received a visit from city coroner, William Murphy, and James Crosbie, asking him to refrain from any military action until the lord mayor and bishop returned to see him on Friday. Unable now to do anything except wait, MacCurtain remained fortified within his headquarters as the heavy fighting continued in Dublin with several British units closing in on the Irish positions. The following day Capt. Dickie met with the lord mayor and Bishop Coholan at the latter's residence to set out the British position which, according to the bishop was that:

> if the arms were given to the Lord Mayor or myself it would be sufficient; that the military authorities would not demand the arms or ask to know where they were kept, but would be satisfied with the word of the Lord Mayor or mine, that he or I was in possession of arms.[32]

The meeting was adjourned until the following night with the lord mayor and bishop agreeing to meet the Volunteer leaders early on Friday morning to convey the British proposal. Bishop Coholan makes no mention of any threat of military action by the British in his account of the meeting with Dickie. However, it is clear from MacCurtain's record that some sort of ultimatum, in which the British threatened to shell their headquarters if they refused to hand up their arms, had been delivered. MacCurtain and his officers however were having none of it: 'We stated at once that we would not, and the sooner the fight started the better'.[33] After discussions lasting three hours, they were prevailed upon by the bishop to accept the terms on offer in principle but sought clarification on the following points:

(1) Whether, if the guns were given in the manner proposed by the military authority, they would be confiscated or remain the property of the Volunteers, to be returned when the crisis was over.
(2) Whether the Volunteers would get an assurance that the subject would be kept out of the papers; that the papers would not be allowed to talk of the disarmament of the Irish Volunteers while other voluntary bodies were allowed to retain theirs.
(3) Would the police would be instructed to cease annoying and irritating individual Volunteers.
(4) Whether the Volunteer leaders would get a permit to visit certain Volunteer centres in Munster with a view to explaining and recommending suggesting the acceptance of the proposal made by the military authority in Cork.[34]

The last query was made in regard to a suggestion put forward by Butterfield that MacCurtain and MacSwiney should use their influence to prevent the outbreak of fighting in other locations in Munster.[35]

These queries were transmitted to General Stafford and later that night Capt. Dickie returned to the bishop's house with the general's reply:

(1) The military have no idea of confiscation, and as far as the military are concerned the arms will be returned once the crisis is over; but the Military cannot speak for Parliament or the civil authority, nor can they give an assurance that a law will not be passed to disarm the Irish Volunteers and all similar associations.
(2) Care would be taken that the papers would not mention the handing in of the rifles
(3) The county inspector of police would be spoken to in order to check the indiscreet zeal of individual policemen.
(4) A permit would be given to the Volunteer leaders to visit, Limerick, Tralee and other districts, to submit to the Volunteers of these centres the Cork agreement, and to counsel acceptance of it.
(5) If these terms were accepted, there should be a general amnesty, unless in the case of persons found in treasonable correspondence with the enemy.[36]

The first point of clarification reflected the reality of the military situation in Dublin where the rebellion was now entering its final stages. Stafford was unable to make any binding agreement since General Sir John Maxwell had on that very day taken over command of all British forces in Ireland and was liable to overturn any action taken by a subordinate officer. The last point was included in response to a personal request made to Stafford by Bishop Coholan without the knowledge of the Volunteers and according to the bishop, the night of Monday 1 May was accepted as the agreed time for handing in the weapons.

Once this agreement was reached Butterfield immediately returned to the Volunteer Hall accompanied this time by Capt. Dickie. There they met face to face with MacCurtain, MacSwiney, and Seán O'Sullivan and the five gathered around the fire in deep discussion until the early hours of the morning. Eventually, at 5 o'clock on Saturday morning the Volunteer leaders, making the best of an untenable situation, reluctantly accepted the terms on offer. Then, and having spent the night without sleep, MacCurtain and MacSwiney left Cork on the eight o'clock train to keep their part of the bargain. They did not know that their colleagues in Dublin were on the verge of surrender or that the *Cork Constitution* was carrying a report claiming that, 'The Cork Sinn Féiners have handed up their rifles to the police'.[37]

This report was a flagrant breach of the terms agreed just hours before and caused considerable unrest amongst the Cork Volunteers. The situation was made worse because MacCurtain and MacSwiney were absent from the city fulfilling their part of the agreement. It was further exacerbated later that night when Capt. Dickie arrived at the Volunteer Hall to see MacCurtain on his return from Limerick. He demanded that the arms be handed up to the lord mayor by midnight on Sunday – and not on Monday as previously agreed. Incensed, MacCurtain refused to hand over anything and the following morning, accompanied by MacSwiney, he again met with the bishop and lord mayor to inform them that under the current circumstances he couldn't ask his men to hand over their arms.

Determined to maintain order in the city, Bishop Coholan persuaded the leaders to put the matter before a general meeting of the Volunteers at 8 o'clock on

Monday night where both he and the lord mayor would address the men. Again left with little option MacCurtain agreed and Coholan and Butterfield again met again with Capt. Dickie to tell him of the latest arrangements. But the captain was far from satisfied and according to the bishop:

> He complained that the terms of the agreement were not kept, that the arms should have been handed in already. I pointed out that according to the [original] agreement 12 o'clock on Monday night was the time limit. I also added that [as] I was going to address the Volunteers in the evening, the time for handing in the arms should be extended to Tuesday night. This was agreed.[38]

A further meeting was scheduled for noon on Monday, which MacCurtain, MacSwiney, Dickie and Coholan were to attend. Neither of the Volunteer officers turned up, but in their absence Dickie and the bishop agreed that the Volunteer arms should be handed over by midnight that night. However later that afternoon Coholan received a phone call from Dickie informing him that all guarantees previously given by the British authorities were now withdrawn. The bishop protested vehemently that this development made it impossible for him to recommend that the Volunteers proceed with the hand over. According to Coholan, as a compromise Dickie stated, 'that though formal guarantees were withdrawn, the arrangements agreed on would go through.'[39] Then accompanied by the lord mayor he made his way to Sheares Street that night to speak to the Volunteers.

Coholan later described the meeting as 'perfectly calm and orderly' and when he addressed the men he never mentioned the fact that the guarantees given in the formal agreement had been withdrawn.[40] Instead he urged them to proceed immediately with the hand over and according to Riobárd Langford, 'there were 120 to 140 men in the Hall and about ninety per cent of those present voted for the surrender'.[41] When the meeting was over some of those who had voted to surrender their arms marched down to the lord mayor's home at 68 South Mall and handed in their weapons. Those who disagreed either retained their arms in secret locations around the city or removed the firing pins to render them unserviceable.[42]

In Dublin that Monday night the city centre was still smouldering from the flames which had engulfed it the previous week and the insurgent Volunteers, together with their Citizen Army and Hibernian Rifle compatriots (including J. J. Walsh), were in military custody. In Cork however all was quiet. While there was intense disappointment within the leadership of the Cork Brigade since they had failed to come to the aid of their comrades in Dublin, there was also consolation to be found in the fact that the week long crisis had been brought to a peaceful conclusion in which they apparently had secured retention of their headquarters, liberty for their men and an understanding that all surrendered weapons would be returned in the near future.

6

Aftermath

Once hostilities had ended nationwide the general expectation within the Cork brigade was that the British authorities would honour the terms of the agreement negotiated by Bishop Coholan and the lord mayor. When General Sir John Maxwell ordered a nationwide crackdown it quickly emerged that Cork would not be treated differently. On Tuesday 2 May the homes of known Volunteers and republicans were raided across the city with MacCurtain, his brother Seán, and nine other Volunteers arrested and incarcerated in the County Gaol.[1] This breach of faith on the part of the British, according to Coholan 'created a bad feeling and a very dangerous excitement in the city'.[2] Although the bishop and lord mayor eventually managed to negotiate the Volunteers' freedom, the release order was later countermanded but those mentioned in it were not re-arrested.

That same day the last major incident of the rebellion occurred and resulted, ironically, in the only fatalities suffered by the Cork Brigade during this period. Early that morning a party of armed RIC constables arrived at the home of the Kent family at Bawnard House, at Castlelyons, County Cork to arrest four Volunteer brothers, Thomas, David, Richard and William. The brothers hadn't received any orders for the rebellion but took the precaution of not sleeping at home until 1 May. With their house surrounded by the RIC the Kents refused to surrender and a gun battle erupted. The fighting lasted for three hours until, with their ammunition expended, the Kents were finally forced to surrender. During the fight Head Constable Rowe was killed and several of his colleagues wounded. David Kent was also seriously injured losing two fingers and receiving a gun-shot wound in his side. After the surrender Richard attempted to escape but was shot and mortally wounded, dying two days later in Fermoy Military Hospital. The remaining brothers were arrested and transported to Cork city, where they were imprisoned in the Military Detention Barracks to await court-martial.

At dawn the following day the execution of the leaders commenced in Dublin with Pearse, Clarke and MacDonagh sent before a firing squad in Kilmainham Jail. In Cork, MacSwiney, Bob and Willie Hales, and two other Volunteers were arrested at the Hales family home in Ballinadee, West Cork.[3] Later that night troops from Victoria Barracks entered the home of the lord mayor and seized and confiscated the weapons which had been deposited there by the Volunteers. To justify this action claims were made by the British that it was the lord mayor himself who had asked Capt. Dickie to remove them on grounds that they were not secure. Butterfield however subsequently refuted this suggestion.[4] For the Volunteers however, the motive for the confiscation was immaterial as the majority of their weapons were now locked away behind the walls of Victoria Barracks.

While the executions continued in Dublin, the Kent brothers were brought before a court-martial in the Detention Barracks. William was acquitted, but both David and Thomas were sentenced to death. David's sentence was eventually commuted to five years penal servitude but Thomas was shot at dawn on the morning of 9 May having requested that no Irishman should be included in his firing squad.

The Kents were not the only Volunteers incarcerated in the Detention Barracks. Capt. Michael Leahy, the officer commanding, the Cobh Company had been arrested with his second-in-command Seamus Fitzgerald at their place of employment in Haulbowline. 'I was asked if I was the leader of the Sinn Féiners,' he later recalled, 'I said, no, I am the leader of the Irish Volunteers'. His interrogator, a British army officer, replied, 'That is good enough for me' and the pair were dragged off to the RIC barracks in Cobh where Liam O'Brien, the company adjutant later joined them.[5] Having refused to disclose any information regarding their weapons, the three were taken to the Military Detention Barracks on 8 May and the following morning were woken from their sleep by the volley of shots which took Thomas Kent's life. After the execution they were again interrogated and Leahy remembered:

> We were told the same fate would be ours. Another argument that was used to endeavour to get us to give up our rifles was that it was pointed out to us that the Cork men had given up theirs and that none of them had been arrested [so] why should we hold out? We continued to refuse to give any information [and] Terence MacSwiney was brought to the Detention Barracks while we were there.[6]

Although MacCurtain remained at liberty he was powerless to intervene and later recorded his anguish at seeing crown forces arrest his fellow Volunteers and take them into custody:

> It was a wretched business that week to be looking at them and hundreds of boys arrested by them. Often I said to myself that it was a great pity that I myself had not been kept in jail when I was there instead of looking at those fine men tied up by them and being brought from every part of the country.[7]

Eventually, MacCurtain's luck ran out, and at 7.15 p.m. on the evening of 11 May the RIC raided his home at 40 Thomas Davis Street and arrested him. Writing later he recalled what happened:

> Siobhan, my wife's sister started to cry when I was leaving the house but Eilis (my wife) did not say a word. She did not want to put any trouble on me along with what I had already and she told me to have courage. This was a great help to me. I kissed Siobhan and Sile and Tomás Óg who was in the cot and went with the peelers ... I was put in the Detention Barracks ... I was searched and everything I had was taken from me except for the copy of the 'Imitation of Christ' that I had in English, it was a very small little book and a great comfort to me – I was put into the cell ... Eilis gave me a glass of milk before I left the house and I was not hungry ... After all the work I was very tired ... I put the board on the floor of my cell and went to sleep.[8]

The following morning MacCurtain got his first taste of life in the Detention Barracks when a bell woke him at 6 a.m. so that he prisoners could wash themselves and have returned to their cells before breakfast and the commencement of a daily routine:

> I was given a mug of some stuff at 8 o'clock and a piece of bread – I think the drink was a mixture of chocolate and cocoa – immediately I had that breakfast eaten a solder came to the door to me and said 'Do not be afraid of anyone here but raise your head and look them between the two eyes'. That encouraged me and lifted the spirit in me and I did so ... We were all let out in the air from 11 to 12 o'clock and a guard of soldiers around us. We would be walking around after one another – about six feet apart and we would not be allowed to say a word to one another. We got a dinner which was not too bad altogether and what we got for breakfast we got again in the evening for supper. We had another 'in the air' between four and five o'clock ... it was in the yard in which we used to walk that Tomás Ceannt was buried after he was shot.[9]

MacCurtain, and the other members of his command, remained in ignorance of their future for the first three weeks of May. Then, On the evening of 21 May they were told to be 'ready for road' the next morning. At 7.30 a.m. on the following day the Volunteers of the Cork Brigade, together with men from other units who had been locked up in Cork, were all handcuffed together in pairs and marched off under military escort to the Great Southern and Western Railway Station on the Lower Glanmire Road. Undaunted by whatever fate awaited them, the Volunteers whistled and sang as they marched down Military Hill, through St Luke's Cross, and down Grattan Hill to the station where a large crowd of terrified relatives and friends had gathered. Amid chaotic scenes of anguish and distress the military escort would not permit any contact between the Volunteers and their loved ones and instead herded the captives on board a train bound for Dublin and detention with their insurgent comrades in Richmond Barracks.

By now fifteen leaders had been executed, and a public outcry had begun to reverberate throughout the country.[10] Afraid of alienating the entire nationalist population and of inflaming pubic opinion in America, the British government were forced to moderate treatment of the insurgents. The executions stopped and instead the Irish rebels were to be interned in Britain. This process commenced almost immediately but in an indication of how the political climate was changing, the Volunteers were cheered as they marched through the streets of Dublin to board the cattle ships that took them into exile.

On arrival in Britain they were sent to a number of different prisons, only to be moved on later that month to an interment camp in Frongoch in North Wales.[11] It was here, in a rat-infested former distillery which up to that point had been used to house German prisoners of war, that the Irish internees established their 'University of Revolution'. Classes soon commenced in Irish history, language and culture, but more importantly, it was here that the leaders of the Cork Brigade used their freedom of association to analyse the failure of the rebellion, and their failure, such as it was, within the overall context. Debating relentlessly by day and by night with other leading Volunteers, like Michael Collins, brought about the realisation that conventional military tactics were no longer appropriate in Ireland given the strength of crown forces operating there. Remaining steadfast in their commitment to fight again, and determined to re-generate the Volunteer organisation and develop it into a credible military force, these internees began planning the next phase of Ireland's struggle for freedom. Internment would not rid the Volunteers of their aspirations – it would only serve to intensify them.

Meanwhile back in Cork those brigade officers who had managed to evade capture were now struggling to keep the unit intact. This became easier in June when some of their men were set free as part of a general release, but most of the leaders, including MacCurtain and MacSwiney, were considered too dangerous and transferred instead to Reading Jail on 11 July. While there they learned that Sir Roger Casement, the man who had addressed the first meeting of the Cork City Corps of Volunteers in December 1913, had been found guilty of treason and was to be hanged at Pentonville Jail in London. At nine o'clock on the morning of 3 August, as the noose tightened on his neck, all Volunteer prisoners in British jails stopped work and recited fifteen decades of the rosary for the repose of Casement's soul.

Throughout his period of incarceration MacCurtain was haunted daily by the events of Easter Week and what he perceived as his own personal failure. Agonising repeatedly over what might have been, and what should have been, he finally arrived at the truth of the matter:

> it is nearly five months ago now and it is many 'a turn' I have had since and my judgement in the matter is that we could not have done otherwise than we did.[12]

MacCurtain could not, and should not, have done other than what he did. Kept in ignorance of the IRB's real intentions until the very last moment, had he chosen to commit his brigade against a far superior force neither he nor many of his colleagues would have lived to fight again. Instead, by offering solid leadership and sound judgement he preserved his force intact and available for future operations. With his soldiers more committed than ever to a cause they all passionately believed in the next phase of Ireland's fight for freedom would be managed in a distinctly different manner. When many of the Volunteers were set free on Christmas Eve 1916 under the terms of a general amnesty they returned home to a heroes' welcome. The next chapter was about to begin and this time the soldiers of the Cork Brigade of Irish Volunteers would play a pivotal role.

Appendix A

Organisation of the Cork Brigade of Irish Volunteers, Easter 1916

By Easter 1916 a total of forty-seven companies of Irish Volunteers had been established within the boundaries of County Cork. Forty-four of these units, with strengths varying from ten men to eighty, formed the Cork Brigade under the command of Tomás MacCurtain, while the remaining three – Charleville, Glanworth and Mitchelstown – were attached to the Galtee Battalion. During the months of September and October 1915 MacCurtain organised twenty-three of his companies into five battalion formations.

Brigade Headquarters – Sheares Street Cork
Brigade Commander – Tomás MacCurtain

1st Battalion (Cork City)
A Company
B Company
C Company
D Company

2nd Battalion
Ballinadee Company
Bandon Company
Clogough Company
Kilbrittain Company

4th Battalion
Ballinagree Company
Carriganimma Company
Clondrohid Company
Kilmurray Company
Kilnamartyra Company

3rd Battalion
Courtbrack Company
Donaghmore Company
Kilmona Company
Mourne Abbey Company
Waterloo Company
Whitechurch Company

5th Battalion
Keale Company
Millstreet Company
Mushera Company
Rathduane Company

Independent Companies
Ahiohill Company
Ardfield Company
Ballingeary Company
Ballinhassig Company
Bantry Company
Boherbue Company
Castletownroche Company
Cobh Company
Dungourney Company
Dunmanway Company
Eyries Company
Gurteen/Tinker's Cross Company
Kanturk Company
Kilpatrick Company
Lyre Company
Macroom Company
Mallow Company
Nadd Company
Reallen & Means Company
Tracton Company
Tullylease Company

Appendix B

List of Irish Volunteers from County Cork deported to Britain in the aftermath of the 1916 Easter Rebellion showing where they were incarcerated and their date of arrival.

Name	Address	Destination	Date
Con Ahern	Main Street, Dunmanway	Wakefield	2 June
Maurice Ahern	Dungourney, Midleton	Wakefield	2 June
Edward Barrett	Kilbrittain, Ballinadee	Wakefield	2 June
Joseph Begley	Castle Road, Bandon	Wakefield	13 May
J. Buckley	High Street, Cork	Wakefield	6 May
William Buckley	Kilcorney,Banteer	Wakefield	13 May
John Callaghan	Cork Road, Bandon	Wakefield	13 May
Patrick Carmody	Millstreet	Wakefield	13 May
William Casey	King Street, Mitchelstown	Wakefield	13 May
Robert Cogan	Allen Villas, Mardyke, Cork	Wakefield	13 May
David Collins	Ballard's Lane, Cork	Wakefield	2 June
Daniel Corkery	Cork Street, Macroom	Wakefield	13 May
John Cronin	Chapel Hill, Macroom	Wakefield	2 June
John Crowley	Glandore, Clonakilty	Wakefield	13 May
William Crowley	Gurteen, Bandon	Wakefield	13 May
Timothy Crowley	Glandore, Clonakilty	Wakefield	13 May
Patrick Deban	Cork Road, Fermoy	Wakefield	13 May
Edward Duggan	Ballyheeda, Ballinhassig	Wakefield	6 May
William Duggan	Dunmanway	Wakefield	2 June
James P. Fitzgerald	East Hill, Queenstown	Wakefield	13 May
Joseph Foley	Ardcluggan, Castletownbere	Wandsworth	2 June
James Franklin	Barrackton, Cork	Wakefield	13 May
John Hales	Knocknacurra, Bandon	Wakefield	13 May
Robert Hales	Knocknacurra, Bandon	Wakefield	13 May
William Hales	Knocknacurra, Bandon	Wakefield	13 May
Christopher Hamilton	Kyle Street, Cork	Wakefield	13 May
Daniel Harrington	Knocksaharing, Macroom	Wakefield	13 May
James Harrington	The Square, Mitchelstown	Wakefield	13 May
M. J. Harris	Tower Street, Cork	Wakefield	2 June
T. F. Harris	Tower Street, Cork	Wakefield	2 June
F. F. Healy	Wilmount House, Cobh	Knutsford	7 June
Mathew Healy	Roughgrove, Bandon	Wakefield	13 May
Laurence Heduvan	Main Street, Charleville	Wakefield	13 May
Daniel J. Hegarty	Fair Street, Mallow	Wakefield	13 May
William Hennessy	Popes Quay, Cork	Wandsworth	2 June
John Hourihan,	Skibbereen	Wakefield	2 June
John Hyde	Saint Finbarr's College, Cork	Wakefield	13 May
Joseph Hyde	Gurteen, Bandon	Wakefield	13 May
Michael Hyde	Ballinhassig	Wakefield	13 May
Patrick Hyde	Knockalucy, Ballinhassig	Wakefield	13 May
Martin Kinery	Patrick Street, Fermoy	Wakefield	13 May
Martin Kinery (Jnr)	Patrick Street, Fermoy	Wakefield	13 May
Michael Leahy	Ballywilliam, Cobh	Wakefield	2 June
Daniel Lordan	Farnalough, Newcestown	Wakefield	13 May
John Lynch	The Bridge, Macroom	Wakefield	13 May
Michael F. Lynch	Grannig, Ballyfeard	Wakefield	2 June
Timothy Lynch	Grannig, Ballyfeard	Wakefield	13 May
Tomás MacCurtain	Thomas Davis Street, Cork	Wakefield	2 June
Daniel McCarthy	East Green, Dunmanway	Knutsford	7 June
John McCarthy	Donoughmore, Timoleague	Wakefield	13 May
William McDonnell	Bandon	Wakefield	13 May
Terence MacSwiney	Gardiner's Tce, Victoria Rd., Cork	Wakefield	2 June

Daniel Manning	Kilbrittain	Wakefield	2 June
Denis Manning	Kilbrittain	Wakefield	2 June
James J. Meade	Kilgarriff, Clonakilty	Wakefield	2 June
William J. Meade	Kilgarriff, Clonakilty	Wakefield	2 June
James Moore	King Street, Fermoy	Glasgow	20 May
Cornelius Murphy	Millstreet	Knutsford	7 June
Eugene Murphy	Barna, Upton	Knutsford	7 June
John Murphy	Crossmahon House, Lissarda	Wakefield	2 June
J. Hogan	Baltimore	Wandsworth	2 June
John Noonan	Ballyfeard	Wakefield	13 May
William Noonan	Ballyfeard	Wakefield	13 May
John O'Brien	Tracton	Wakefield	13 May
Seán O'Brien	Clancy Street, Fermoy	Wakefield	13 May
William O'Brien	Tracton	Wakefield	13 May
William O'Brien	The Beach, Queenstown	Wakefield	13 May
Cornelius O'Callaghan	Mill Road, Millstreet	Wandsworth	2 June
Christopher O'Connell	Beecher Street, Mallow	Wakefield	13 May
Patrick O'Connor	New Street, Macroom	Wakefield	13 May
Stephen O'Connor	New Street, Macroom	Wakefield	13 May
Seán O'Deagha	Rathluirc	Wakefield	2 June
W. O'Doherty	Shamrock Terrace, Blarney	Stafford	1 May
Cornelius O'Donoghue	Ballinadee	Knutsford	16 June
Daniel O'Donoghue	Rathdrought, Bandon	Wandsworth	2 June
Patrick O'Donoghue	Ballinadee	Knutsford	16 June
John O'Donovan	Casheliskey, Clonakilty	Wakefield	13 May
Peter O'Donovan	Clonakilty	Wakefield	13 May
Thomas O'Driscoll	Bandon	Wakefield	13 May
J. B. O'Driscoll	Castletownsend	Wakefield	2 June
Patrick O'Dwyer	Hill Terrace, Bandon	Wakefield	13 May
John O'Halloran	Ballingeary	Wakefield	13 May
Tim O'Halloran	Ballingeary	Wakefield	13 May
Peter O'Hourihane	Skibbereen	Wakefield	2 June
Eugene O'Keeffe	Courlea, Clonakilty	Knutsford	2 June
John O'Leary	Clonakilty	Wandsworth	2 June
John O'Leary	Ballinhassig	Wakefield	13 May
James O'Leary	Rossmore, Ballineen	Wakefield	13 May
Con O'Mahoney	Ahiohill, Enniskeane	Wakefield	2 June
Joseph O'Reilly	Chapel Street, Bantry	Stafford	1 May
Patrick O'Shea	King Street, Fermoy	Wakefield	13 May
Timothy O'Shea	Dunmanway	Wakefield	2 June
Patrick O'Sullivan	Bank Place, Mitchelstown	Wakefield	13 May
Michael Quill	Douglas Street, Cork	Lewes	20 May
John Reardon	Macroom	Wakefield	13 May
Tim Reardon	Ballinhassig	Wakefield	13 May
Jeremiah Riordan	Millstreet	Wakefield	13 May
Michael Riordan	Millstreet	Wakefield	13 May
John Roche	Knocknacurra, Bandon	Wakefield	13 May
Michael Savage	Kilshannig, Fermoy	Wakefield	13 May
Timothy Sexton	Skaif, Timoleague	Knutsford	7 June
John Spillane	Castlelyons, Fermoy	Wakefield	13 May
Cornelius Sullivan	Presbytery, Dunmanway	Knutsford	7 June
Edward Sullivan	Clonakilty	Wakefield	13 May
J. Twomey	Millstreet	Wakefield	13 May
Richard Twomey	Ballymountain, Bandon	Wakefield	13 May
D. Walsh	Gaggan, Bandon	Glasgow	20 May
James Walsh	Knockey	Wakefield	13 May
Michael Walsh	Rathroon, Bandon	Knutsford	2 June
Redmond Walsh	Kilmore, Bandon	Wakefield	13 May
Mark Wickham	Merchant's Quay, Cork	Wakefield	13 May

Published Works

Browne, Charles, *The History of the 7th* (Macroom nd)

Chavasse, Moirin, *Terence MacSwiney* (Clonmore & Reynolds Ltd 1961)

Connolly, S. J., ed., *The Oxford Companion to Irish History* (Oxford University Press, 1998)

Costello, Francis J. *Enduring the Most: The Life and Death of Terence MacSwiney* (Dingle, 1995)

Duggan, John P., *A History of the Irish Army* (Gill & Macmillan Ltd Dublin 1991)

Feeney, P. J., *Glory O, Glory O, Ye Bold Fenian Men – A History of the Sixth Battalion, Cork First Brigade 1913–1921* (Dripsey 1996)

Hart, Peter, *The I.R.A. & Its Enemies – Violence and Community in Cork 1916–1923* (Oxford University Press 1998)

Harvey, Dan and White, Gerry, *The Barracks – A History of Victoria/Collins Barracks, Cork* (Mercier Press, 1997)

Hickey, D. J., and Doherty, J. E., ed., *A New Dictionary of Irish History From 1800* (Gill and MacMillan, Dublin 2003)

Horgan, John J., *Parnell to Pearse – Some Recollections and Reflections* (Browne and Nolan Ltd, Dublin, 1948)

Lee, J. J., *Ireland 1912 – 1925 Politics and Society* (Cambridge University Press 1989)

Macardle, Dorothy, *The Irish Republic* (Irish Press ltd, Dublin 1951)

Martin, F. X., ed., *The Irish Volunteers 1913-1915 – Recollections and Documents* (James Duffy & Co. Dublin, 1963)

Moody, T. W. and Martin, F. X., *The Course of Irish History* (Mercier Press, Cork 1967)

Norway, M. L. & A. H., *The Sinn Féin Rebellion as they saw it* (Irish Academic Press, Dublin 1999)

O'Connor, Frank, *An Only Child* (The Blackstaff Press Ltd, Belfast 1993)

O'Donoghue, Florence, *Tomás MacCurtain* (Anvil Books, 1955)

O'Hegarty, P. S., *A Short Memoir of Terence MacSwiney* (The Talbot Press Dublin 1924)

O'Hegarty, P. S., *The Victory of Sinn Féin* (University College Dublin Press Dublin 1998)

Rebel Cork's Fighting Story (Tralee n.d.)

Ryan, Meda, *Tom Barry: Irish Freedom Fighter* (Mercier Press, Cork 2004)

Ryle Dwyer, T., *Tans, Terror and Troubles – Kerry's Real Fighting Story 1913–23* (Mercier Press, Cork 2001)

White, Gerry and O'Shea, Brendan, *The Irish Volunteer Soldier 1913–1923* (Osprey Publishing UK 2003)

Periodicals

An Cosantoir
Journal of the Cork Historical and Archaeological Society
Capuchin Annual
Cork Holly Bough
The Irish Volunteer

Newspapers

Cork Examiner
Cork Constitution
Cork Free Press
Evening Echo
Freeman's Journal
Irish Times
Irish Independent

Manuscript Collections

Cork Public Museum
Tomás MacCurtain Papers
Terence MacSwiney Papers
Michael Leahy Papers

Cork Archives Institute
Seamus Fitzgerald Papers
Riobárd Langford Papers
Liam de Róiste Papers

Irish Military Archives
Bureau of Military History Collection

National Library of Ireland
Florence O'Donoghue Papers

Private Collections
Seán Murphy Papers
Con Meaney Papers

Unpublished Works

Girvan, Kevin Edward, *The Life and Times of Seán O'Hegarty (1881to1963) O/C First Cork Brigade War of Independence*, Mphil Thesis (Cork, 2003)

Notes

1 – Origins

1 Born in Kilrane, County Wexford in 1856, John Redmond was first elected to parliament for New Ross in 1881. He soon established himself within the party as an able administrator, fund-raiser and lieutenant of Parnell. After Parnell's death in 1891 he led the pro-Parnell faction of the party until 1900 when he was elected leader of the re-unified party.

2 Formed by Michael Cusack and Maurice Davin on 1 November 1884 at a meeting held in the billiard room of Hayes Hotel, Thurles, County Tipperary

3 Established in Dublin on 31 July 1893 by Douglas Hyde, Eoin MacNeill (who became the League's first secretary) and Fr Eugene O'Growney.

4 From *Memoirs of Eoin MacNeill,* unpublished – quoted in *The Irish Volunteers 1913–1915*, Martin, F. X., ed., James Duffy & Co. Ltd, Dublin 1963, p. 72.

5 Martin, F. X., ed., *The Irish Volunteers 1913–1915 Recollections and Document*, pp. 110–111.

6 *The Irish Times*, 26 November 1913.

7 At constituency level the Irish Parliamentary Party was initially known as the Irish National League.

8 Charles Stewart Parnell was MP for Cork from 1880 to 1891.

9 In March 1891 the anti-Parnell majority seceded from the Irish National League and set up its own constituency body, The Irish National Federation led by Justin MacCarthy and John Dillon while the pro-Parnellites led by John Redmond retained control of the League.

10 William O'Brien was born in Mallow County Cork in 1852 and following his education at Queen's College Cork became a journalist working on *The Cork Daily Herald* from 1868–76 and the *Freeman's Journal* from 1876–81. He was also a well known land agitator and member of the Land League and in 1881 he was imprisoned with Parnell. On his release he became the main organiser of the National League and in 1887 became MP for North-East Cork. In 1892 he was elected as MP for Cork and during the party crisis of 1889–90 he declined an invitation from Parnell to replace Justin MacCarthy as chairman of the party. After Parnell's death in 1891 he became a founding member of the Irish National Federation. Appalled by a famine in Mayo in 1898 he founded the United Irish League which became instrumental in re-uniting the Irish Party under John Redmond in 1900.

11 Formed in America in 1836 as an Irish American benevolent organisation and in Ireland in1838 as a Catholic reaction to the Orange Order. It soon became the largest Irish society in America but split in 1878 over the decision taken about the admission of members of Irish descent rather than Irish birth. The organisation remained divided until the 1902 conference established the Board of Erin in an attempt to heal the rift. A majority within the AOH (around 60,000 members) agreed to reconciliation but a minority of some 6,000 refused to accept its authority. The AOH (Board of Erin) went on to become major supporters of the Irish Parliamentary Party.

12 O'Connor, Frank, *An Only Child*, Macmillan and Company Ltd. 1961, p. 6.

13 Born in Dublin in 1871, Griffith was a printer and journalist. In October 1893 he formed the Celtic Literary Society with William Rooney in order to study Irish language, history, literature and music. He was also a member of the Gaelic League and IRB, an advocate of economic self-sufficiency and a political system based on a 'Dual Monarchy' of Britain and Ireland similar to that of Austria-Hungary. In 1899 he founded the *United Irishman* newspaper which became the official organ of Cumann na nGaedheal. On the formation of the Sinn Féin party he founded a journal of the same name to promote party policy.

14 William Rooney was a journalist and language activist who was born in Dublin in 1871. A member of the Gaelic league he was also instrumental with Arthur Griffith in founding the Celtic Literary Society and Cumann na nGaedheal.

15 The founding members of the Cork Literary Society were Terence MacSwiney, Fred Cronin, Dan Tierney, Bob Fitzgerald and Liam de Róiste

16 Inghinidhe na hÉireann (Daughters of Ireland) was a national separatist movement for women founded by Maud Gonne MacBride in April 1900.

17 The Dungannon Club was republican organisation founded in Belfast on 8 March 1905 in commemoration of the 1782 Volunteer convention at Dungannon County Tyrone.

18 Seán O'Hegarty was born in Cork city on 21 March 1881. At an early age he developed a passion for the language and culture of Ireland and joined the Gaelic League after the first branch was established in Cork in 1899. At beginning of the century, the IRB organisation in Cork consisted of

a number of elderly men. In 1906, the Supreme Council of the IRB, at the recommendation of P. S. O'Hegarty (Seán's brother) decided to form a new 'Circle' in Cork consisting of younger men and O'Hegarty became its leader or 'Centre'.

19 Original letter in De Róiste Papers, Cork Archives Institute, ref: U271/E/2.

20 De Róiste Diary, Cork Archives Institute, ref: U271/A/16.

21 *Ibid.*

22 *Account of the formation of Cork Corps of Irish Volunteers* written by Diarmuid Fawsitt, Cork Archives Institute, ref: U/265.

23 Walsh, J. J, Witness Statement no. 91, The Bureau of Military History, Military Archives.

24 In August 1913 the Cunard Line broke their contract to land the eastbound mails at Queenstown because they considered the port unsafe for their new liners, the *Lusitania* and *Mauretania*.

25 De Róiste Diary, Cork Archives Institute, ref: U271/A/16.

26 *Ibid.*

27 Now Kent Station on the Lower Glanmire Road, Cork.

28 De Róiste Diary, Cork Archives Institute, ref: U271/A/16.

29 Horgan, John J., *Parnell to Pearse*, Browne and Nolan Ltd, 1948, p. 226

30 *Ibid.*, p. 227

31 De Róiste Diary, Cork Archives Institute, ref: U271/A/16.

32 Tomás MacCurtain was born at Ballyknockane, County Cork on 20 March 1884. When he was thirteen years old he came to Cork city to live with his older sister at 68 Great Britain Street. He completed his education at the North Monastery where he developed a passion for the Irish language and in 1901 joined the Blackpool branch of the Gaelic League – Craobh na Linne Duibhe. Having left school MacCurtain secured employment as a clerk with the Cork Steampacket Company but he was persuaded to leave to take up full time employment as a teacher and organiser with the Gaelic League. His work for the League took him to parts of Limerick and south Tipperary where he remained until 1907 when he returned to Cork to take up a position at Mack's Mill in Crosses Green. In 1906 he was inducted into the Cork city 'Circle' of the Irish Republican Brotherhood and the following year he joined the Cork branch of the National Council of Sinn Féin where he served as a member of the Executive Committee from November 1909 to 1911. In 1908 he married Eilis Walsh, a fellow member of the Blackpool Branch of the Gaelic League. He formed the Cork Branch of Fianna Éireann in 1911 and that same year joined the National Vigilance Committee formed to oppose a loyal address by Cork Corporation to the King of England.

33 Terence MacSwiney was born at North Main Street, Cork city on 28 March 1879. Following his education at the North Monastery he secured employment at Dwyer & Co., a Cork warehouse and distribution firm. Though employed full time, he continued to study for a degree in philosophy that he obtained in 1907. From an early age he developed a love for the Irish language and culture and on 2 January 1901, was a founder member of the Cork Literary Society which had its headquarters at 31 Great George's Street (now Washington Street). Subsequent to the visit of King Edward VII to Cork in 1903, MacSwiney drafted a circular on behalf of the society calling on 'all self-respecting Irishmen' to refrain from any participation in welcoming ceremonies for the English king. In 1908 he became a member of the Cork Dramatic Society. By the time of the inaugural meeting of the Cork Branch of the Volunteers, Terence MacSwiney was totally committed to the cause of Irish freedom.

34 Riobárd Langford's account of the meeting (Langford Papers – Cork Archives Institute ref: U/156) lists Seán O'Hegarty as being present on the platform though he is not mentioned either by de Róiste, Fawsitt or Walsh.

35 *Cork Examiner*, Monday 15 December 1913

36 *Ibid.*

37 Fawsitt, Diarmuid, *Cork Corps of Irish Volunteers*, Cork Archives Institute, ref: U/265.

38 *Ibid.*

39 *Cork Examiner*, Monday 15 December 1913.

40 De Róiste Diary, Cork Archives Institute, ref: U271/A/16.

41 Fawsitt, Diarmuid, *Cork Corps of Irish Volunteers*, Cork Archives Institute, ref: U/265.

42 *Ibid.*

43 Walsh, John J., *Recollections of a Rebel*, p. 24.

44 De Róiste Diary, Cork Archives Institute, ref: U271/A/16.

45 *Ibid.*

46 Fawsitt, Diarmuid, *Cork Corps of Irish Volunteers*, Cork Archives Institute, ref: U/265.

47 De Róiste Diary, Cork Archives Institute, ref: U271/A/16.

48 Born in Ballyglass, County Mayo in 1854, Maurice Moore was commissioned in the British army in 1875 and fought in the Kaffir and Zulu Wars of 1877–79. He was commanding officer of the 1st Battalion, the Connaught Regiment, from 1900–06 and formed a cavalry corps that fought with distinction in the Boer War. He was a staunch supporter of the Irish Parliamentary Party and Home Rule.

49 A native of Ballyglass, County Mayo where he was born in 1811, George Moore was MP for County Mayo from 1847–57. An excellent landlord and supporter of tenant's rights Moore was the founder of the Catholic Defence Association and a founding member of the Independent Irish Party. He regained his seat in 1868 and retained it until his death in 1870 and was the father of Colonel Maurice Moore and the novelist George Moore.

50 Fawsitt, Diarmuid, *Cork Corps of Irish Volunteers*, Cork Archives Institute, ref: U/265.

51 Compiled from two entries in the de Róiste diaries: 24/11/14 and 8/12/14. Cork Archives Institute, ref: U271/A/16.

52 In a letter printed in the *Cork Examiner* on Tuesday, 16 December 1914, de Róiste stated that 'about 500 names were enrolled' while Roger Casement in a letter printed in the *Cork Examiner* on Wednesday, 17 December 1914 said that 'some 700 names were given in'.

53 Ruiseal, Liam, 'The Position in Cork', in *The Capuchin Annual*, 1966.

54 *Cork Examiner*, Tuesday 16 December.

55 *Ibid.*, Monday 15 December 1913.

56 *Ibid.*, Tuesday 16 December 1913.

57 *Ibid.*, Thursday 18 December 1913

58 *Ibid*

59 O'Hegarty, P. S., *A Short Memoir of Terence MacSwiney*, The Talbot Press Dublin, p. 45.

2 – Expansion

1 De Róiste Diary, Cork Archives Institute, ref: U271/A/16.

2 O'Hegarty, P. S., *A Short Memoir of Terence MacSwiney*, p. 46–47.

3 Walsh, John J., *Recollections of a Rebel*, p. 24.

4 In 1913 the IRB members in Cobh were Michael Leahy, Liam O'Brien and Patrick Curran.

5 Statement by Michael Leahy, in Seamus Fitzgerald Papers, Cork Archives Institute, ref: no. PR/6/40.

6 Quoted *in Glory O, Glory O, Ye Bold Fenian Men, A History of the Sixth Battalion, Cork First Brigade 1913–21*, by P. J. Feeney (Dripsey 1996).

7 Meaney, Cornelius, Witness Statement no. 64, Bureau of Military History, Military Archives.

8 Martin, F. X., ed., *The Irish Volunteers 1913–1915*, p. 133.

9 *Ibid.*

10 *Ibid*, p. 134.

11 *Ibid.*, p. 133.

12 Walsh, John J., *Recollections of a Rebel*, p. 27. Walsh refers to a 'Captain Lindsey Talbot Crosbie' but the officer in question was in fact his son, Maurice Talbot Crosbie.

13 Martin, F. X., ed., *The Irish Volunteers 1913–1915*, p. 45. According to Bulmer Hobson the decision to hold a National Convention 'was made at the suggestion of MacNeill, but it certainly did not arise out of any report by him on discussions with Redmond, for he did not make any such report'.

14 MacNeill initially proposed an Executive Committee of six: MacNeill, J. Gore, Lawrence Kettle, The O'Rahilly, Sir Roger Casement and William Redmond. Redmond accepted these names but insisted on adding a further two to be nominated by him. In a letter to Redmond on 23 May MacNeill agreed but suggested the inclusion of Colonel Maurice Moore. Redmond accepted this proposal and named his two nominees as Michael Davitt and Joseph Devlin. Davitt however was unacceptable to MacNeill and he informed Redmond of this by letter on 29 May. Redmond countered by writing to MacNeill on 3 June that he understood that he [MacNeill] no longer desired his co-operation or that of his friends in controlling the Volunteers and that he would now act accordingly.

15 *Irish Independent*, 9 June 1914.

16 *Cork Examiner*, 13 June 13 1915.

17 Martin, F. X., ed., *The Irish Volunteers 1913–1915*, p. 143.

18 *Ibid*, p. 144. The letter issued to the press was only signed by eight members: Eamon Ceannt, M. J. Judge, Con Ó Colbaird, John Fitzgibbon, Eamon Martin, P. H. Pearse, Seán MacDermott and Piaras Beaslaí. Liam Mellows voted against the motion but his name does not appear on the letter.

19 O'Donoghue, Florence, *Tomás MacCurtain – Soldier and Patriot*, Anvil Books, Tralee 1955, p. 36.

20 *Cork Examiner*, 22 June 1914.

21 In his biography of Tomás MacCurtain, Florence O'Donoghue wrote that in subsequent parades and marches 'The green flag was the only one displayed' and 'it does not appear that the city arms flag was ever used'.

22 De Róiste Papers, Cork Archives Institute, ref: U271/E/3 (vii).

23 These weapons had actually been unloaded from O'Brien's yacht off Bardsley Island off the Welsh coast and transferred to one belonging to Sir Myles O'Brien, a prominent Dublin surgeon who subsequently took them ashore.

24 O'Donoghue, Florence, *Tomás MacCurtain*, p. 38.

3 – Division

1 *Cork Examiner*, 1 August 1914.

2 *Ibid.*

3 *Ibid.*

4 *Ibid.*

5 *Ibid.*

6 O'Donoghue, Florence, *Tomás MacCurtain*, p. 39. A report in the *Cork Constitution* of 4 August made no mention of the ship being detained: 'The moon was up and shone upon the scene so brightly that the naval patrol which guards the region of "Carbery's Hundred Isles" had no difficulty in seeing the ship and rifles making for Baltimore and induced it change its course and make for the open sea'.

7 *Cork Constitution*, 4 August 1914.

8 *Ibid.*

9 Ruiseal, Liam, 'The Situation in Cork', p. 373.

10 *Cork Constitution*, 5 August 1914.

11 *Ibid.*

12 O'Donoghue, Florence, *Tomás MacCurtain*, p. 42.

13 *Cork Constitution*, 6 August 1914.

14 *Cork Examiner* and *Cork Constitution*, 8 August 1914.

15 *Cork Constitution*, 8 August 1914. In his account of this meeting which appeared in part 27 of 'Mar Is Cuimin Liom' in *The Evening Echo* on 18 November 1954, Liam de Róiste, 'The majority of those present were the supporters of Mr Redmond who had joined the Corps after the Parliamentary Party expressed support for the Volunteers. They were silent on Capt. Crosbie's pronouncements. But there were murmurings and loud dissent from those who had founded and formed the Cork Volunteers. They felt they were being betrayed by their commanding officer. It was not to help the British Government they had enrolled in the Volunteers.'

16 Accounts of these scenes are carried in all Cork newspapers during the month of August 1914.

17 *Cork Examiner*, 11 August 1914.

18 *Cork Examiner*, 12 August 1914.

19 *Cork Constitution*, 11 August 1914.

20 *Cork Examiner*, 17 August 1914.

21 *Cork Constitution*, 29 August 1914.

22 De Róiste, Liam, 'Mar Is Cuimin Liom, part 28, in *The Evening Echo*, 20 November 1954.

23 *Ibid.*

24 According to the original minutes of this meeting held in the Cork Public Museum (ref: no. L. 1963. 85) this resolution was a composite one compiled from a motion proposed by Fawsitt suspending Talbot Crosbie from membership of the executive and one proposed by Seán O'Hegarty demanding his removal from the appointments he held.

25 Original document in de Róiste Papers, Cork Archives Institute, ref: U/271/E.

26 De Róiste, Liam, 'Mar Is Cuimin Liom', part 28.

27 Walsh, J. J., *Recollections of a Rebel*, p. 28.

28 *Cork Examiner*, 31 August 1914.

29 *Ibid.*

30 Walsh, J. J., *Recollections*, p. 28.

31 De Róiste in 'Mar Is Cuimin Liom' part 28 states that the figure was 'between seventy or eighty' while O'Donoghue in his biography of MacCurtain states that, 'between fifty and sixty men, including all of the officers, with the exception of Talbot Crosbie' supported the executive.

32 *Cork Examiner*, 31 August 1914.

33 *Ibid.*

34 Girvan, Kevin, *The Life and Times of Seán O'Hegarty*, MPhil Thesis (Cork, 2003), p. 35.

35 He was subsequently appointed postmaster at Walshpool North Wales.

36 Walsh, J. J. *Recollections*, p. 34.

37 Langford Papers, Cork Archives Institute, ref. U156.

38 *Cork Examiner*, 3 September 1914.

39 O'Donoghue, Florence; *Tomás MacCurtain*, p.48.

40 *Ibid.*

41 This account of the Executive Committee meeting is taken from p. 49 of O'Donoghue's biography of MacCurtain. Why Talbot Crosbie would deny that he had resigned is not clear as he had already made known his intentions to re-join the British army and in October 1914 he was appointed as an officer in the Royal Artillery.

42 *Cork Examiner*, 14 September 1914.

43 *Ibid.*

44 Chavasse, Moirin, *Terence MacSwiney*, Clonmore and Reynolds Ltd, Dublin 1961, p. 36.

45 *Fianna Fáil*, Issue 1, 19 September 1914 – in Cork Public Museum.

46 *Cork Constitution*, 21 September 1914.

47 Martin, F. X., ed., *The Irish Volunteers 1913–1915*, pp. 153–155.

48 *Ibid.*

49 Voting list is taken from p. 210 of O'Donoghue's biography of MacCurtain. Walsh is shown as present on this occasion and at a further meeting held on 3 October. However Walsh's memoirs and other documentation, including a manifesto drawn up by the Provisional Committee in October 1914 states that after the Cornmarket parade of 6 September Walsh was given twenty-four hours to leave Ireland. It is our view that while Walsh had been ordered to leave and had agreed to do so he was still preparing to leave at the time this meeting was held and departed for Bradford shortly afterwards.

50 O'Donoghue, Florence, *Tomás MacCurtain*, p. 51.

51 While the Irish name of the Volunteer movement was 'Óglaigh na hÉireann' from its inception, both variants of the English name, i.e. 'Irish Volunteers' and 'Irish National Volunteers', had also been used on official documentation from the beginning. After the split both bodies of Volunteers could therefore argue that they retained the 'official' title of the organisation.

4 – Reorganisation

1 Langford Papers, Cork Archives Institute, ref. U 156.

2 Horgan, John J., *Parnell to Pearse – Some Recollections and Reflections*, Browne and Nolan Ltd. Dublin, 1948, p. 264.

3 De Róiste, Liam, 'Mar Is Cuimin Liom', part 29 in *The Evening Echo* 25 November 1954.

4 *Cork Constitution*, 3 October 1914.

5 Minutes of meeting in Cork Public Museum, ref. L. 1963. 85.

6 O'Donoghue, Florence; *Tomás MacCurtain*, p.51.

7 *Minutes of National Volunteers, Lord Carbery Branch 1914–1918*, Cork Archives Institute, ref. U279.

8 *Ibid.*

9 *Cork Examiner*, 3 October 1914.

10 *Cork Examiner*, 5 October 1914.

11 *Ibid.*

12 *Ibid.*

13 *Ibid.*

14 *Ibid.*

15 *Ibid.*

16 *Ibid.* The meeting elected new officers and a committee of eight with one member to represent the Cycle Corps. Those elected officers were: Chairman, Thomas Byrne; Honorary Secretaries, J. Mullane, and E. Gaynor TC; Honorary Treasurers; John J. Horgan, J. J. McEnry and Joseph Murphy T.C. Those elected to the committee were: J. Bradley, H. P. F. Donegan, George Crosbie, J. Hoare, D. Lehane, R. Carlisle, J. Conway, J. F. O'Riordan with P. Egan representing the Cycle Corps.

17 John J. Horgan also donated two new colours for the corps.

18 Girvan, Kevin, *The Life and Times of Seán O'Hegarty* p. 36 and Norway, M.L. & A. H, *The Sinn Féin*

Rebellion as they saw it (Irish Academic Press, Dublin 1999), p. 102

19 O'Donoghue, Florence, *Tomás MacCurtain*, pp.54–55.

20 Ruiseal, Liam, 'The Situation in Cork', in the *Capuchin Annual*, 1966, pp. 373.

21 A limited number of leaflets containing the Manifesto were eventually distributed.

22 De Róiste Papers, Cork Archives Institute, ref: U/271/E/ (v).

23 Martin, F. X., ed., *The Irish Volunteers 1913–1915*, p. 159.

24 The proposed constitution of the Irish Volunteers, passed at a meeting of the Provisional Committee, originally made provision for a General Council comprising 50 members – one delegate from each of the thirty-two counties and one from the cities of Dublin, Belfast, Cork, Limerick, Derry, Waterford, Galway, Sligo and Kilkenny and nine members other than the delegates direct, resident within ten miles of the city of Dublin. At the convention however twenty-one members of the original Provisional Committee were unanimously re-elected to the General Council which, together with the county and city delegates, now totalled sixty-two.

25 *The Irish Volunteer*, 31 October 1914. The convention also reaffirmed the aims and objectives of the movement in the following policy which was proposed by MacNeill and unanimously passed: 1. To maintain the right and duty of the Irish nation henceforward to provide for its own defence by means of a permanent armed and trained Volunteer force. 2. To unite the people of Ireland on the basis of Irish Nationality and a common national interest; to maintain the integrity of the nation and to resist with all our strength any measures tending to bring about or perpetuate disunion or the partition of our country. 3. To resist any attempt to force the men of Ireland into military service under any Government until a free National Government of Ireland is empowered by the Irish people themselves to deal with it. 4. To secure the abolition of the system of governing Ireland through Dublin Castle and the British military power, and the establishment of a National Government in its place.

26 *Cork Examiner*, 23 November 1914.

27 Liam de Róiste Diary, Cork Archives Institute, ref: U271/A/16.

28 Allen, Larkin and O'Brien were found guilty of the murder of police sergeant Charles Brett who was killed during the attack on a prison wagon carrying the Fenian leaders Thomas J. Kelly and Timothy Deasy, at Hyde Road, Manchester on 18 September 1867.

29 Liam de Róiste Diary, Cork Archives Institute, ref: U271/A/16.

30 *Cork Examiner*, 30 November 1914.

31 Born in Westport, County Mayo in 1865 John MacBride became a member the IRB in the 1880s and later joined the Celtic Literary Society. MacBride befriended Arthur Griffith and soon became disillusioned with the IRB and having returned from a mission to the USA he emigrated to South Africa and became an assayer for the Rand Mining Company. On the outbreak of the Boer War, he organised an Irish brigade to fight with the Boers. After the war he returned to Ireland where Griffith introduced him to Maud Gonne, who subsequently converted to Catholicism allowing the couple to marry on 21 February 1903. The following year they had one son, Seán, but the marriage ended in judicial separation in 1905. MacBride also secured a position on Dublin corporation and was vice-president of Cumann na nGaedheal and was a member of the National Council and Sinn Féin.

32 De Róiste, Liam, 'Mar Is Cuimin Liom', part 30, in *The Evening Echo* on 27 November 1954.

33 *Cork Examiner*, 30 November 1914.

34 *Ibid.*

35 *Ibid.*

36 *Ibid.*

37 *Ibid.*, 2 December 1914.

38 The *Cork Examiner*, 3 December 1914: 'Considering the good feeling which prevails in Cork between both bodies of Volunteers we regret that the circular by many inaccurate statements seems designed to provoke controversy ... A full explanation in connection with this matter was given to the executive of the corps of which at that time Messers. George Crosbie, B.L., J. F. O'Riordan T.C., solr., and Thomas Byrne were members. Prior to the secession it was decided by the then executive, on the suggestion of the Hon. Treasurers, to have the accounts audited. This was done in due course by Messers. Stapleton and Co., charters accountants Cork. The accounts so audited have been published. It can be seen from the published accounts the uses to which the monies subscribed by the public were put. It is stated in the circular to which we refer that £600 was sent "to Mr Mac-Neill's Committee in Dublin". There was no such committee in existence at that time. This sum of

money was sent to headquarters, Dublin before the division in the ranks took place and in accordance with the public announcements regarding the Defence of Ireland Fund. The money was sent for the purchase of rifles for the Cork Corps. On the application of Mr Thomas Byrne £100 was sent to Mr John E. Redmond M.P., for a like purpose. One hundred rifles were received in return for this money. These rifles were subsequently stolen from the headquarters Fisher Street and are now, we understand, in the possession of Mr Redmond's Volunteers in Cork. In a paragraph which appears in today's "Examiner" it is stated that the corps under Mr Redmond's presidency "received no benefit from the collections made in the city in July". We have shown that this statement is not accurate. It is said in the circular that the executive of the Cork City Corps Irish Volunteers "studiously prevented a free ballot of Volunteers". This statement is absolutely untrue. It is also said that "these gentlemen who had never really represented the rank and file were bent on pursuing a policy calculated to injure both the country and the Volunteers". In reply to this statement we wish to point out that 'the gentlemen' referred to in the circular were the men who founded the Volunteers in Cork, when those who now criticise them endeavoured to smash the Volunteer movement. It may interest the citizens to know that at present no rifles for Volunteers in Ireland can be procured. The English Government has stopped the importation of military stores into this country, and has procured from every merchant in Ireland a return of all such stores held by him. The intention obviously is to prevent the arming and equipping of the Irish Volunteers.'

39 Ibid., 4 December 1914.

40 Ibid.

41 Liam de Róiste Diary, Cork Archives Institute, ref: U271/A/16.

42 Cork Examiner, 8 December 1914.

43 Ibid., 9 December 1914.

44 Ibid., 14 December 1914.

45 In the same letter de Róiste also stated that the bulk of the money collected for the Defence of Ireland Fund had been collected before the City Hall meeting. He went on to say that Horgan never had, or claimed to have had, control over this money, or the ordinary funds, and that the only money he [Horgan] claimed to have had a role in the disposal of disposing the sums subscribed at the meeting of 31 July or received as a direct result of that event. This money comprised one-fourth of the total sum forwarded to the fund. De Róiste also confirmed that on 10 September, with the exception of the £100 that was sent to Redmond to purchase weapons, the whole amount of money that Horgan claimed to have control of was lodged in the bank.

46 Cork Examiner, 14 December 1914.

47 Cork Examiner, 16 December 1914.

48 Other publications suppressed at this time were Sinn Féin, Irish Freedom, The Irish Worker, Ireland, and The Cork Celt. Arthur Griffith replied to this action by publishing a small paper called Scissors and Paste which contained no leading article and was comprised mainly of cuttings from foreign newspapers.

49 De Róiste, Liam, 'Mar Is Cuimin Liom', part 31, in The Evening Echo, 21 November 1954.

50 Ibid.

51 Horgan, John J., Parnell to Pearse, p. 266 – from a speech made by Lloyd George in the House of Commons on 18 October 1916.

52 Seven nationalist MPs ultimately enlisted in the British army – six from the Irish Party: Willie Redmond (John Redmond's brother), William Archer Redmond (John Redmond's son), Dr John Esmonde, his son John Lymrick Esmonde, Stephen Gwynn and Arthur Lynch, and an O'Brienite, D. D. Sheehan.

53 Horgan, John J., Parnell to Pearse, p. 266.

54 Ibid., p. 267.

55 Cork Free Press, 6 January 1915.

56 Horgan, John J., Parnell to Pearse, pp. 268–269.

57 On 4 February Brigadier-General Cecil Hill, the officer commanding South Irish Coast Defence wrote a letter to RIC County Inspector Howe from his headquarters in Queenstown:
Dear Mr Howe, – The G.O.C. in Ireland has had under consideration the question of the guarding of the railway bridges over the River Lee by an armed guard of the National Volunteers and requests that you will be so good as to inform them as follows. While fully acknowledging the patriotic spirit which has lead them to offer their services and thanking them for services already rendered, he finds it impossible to continue their employment as an armed guard. If they are willing to continue to give

their services as an unarmed guard in the nature of special constables he will gladly accept their offer to guard the bridges which they have been guarding, and in any other capacity in which the garrison commander should require their services. I am directed to add that it is not considered possible to allow citizens who do not belong to the armed forces of the crown to bear arms in the defence of the realm.

Howe forwarded this letter to Capt. Donegan of the National Volunteers who replied on 6 February:

Dear Mr Howe – I have yours of 6th enclosing General Hill's letter from which I note that the G.O.C. in Ireland directs the discontinuance of the armed guard furnished by the Cork city regiment of the Irish National Volunteers since 1st January last, and that if the men are willing to give their services as an unarmed guard in the nature of special constables he will gladly accept their offer to guard the bridges which they have been guarding, or in any other capacity in which the Garrison commander shall require. I desire to say that while guarding the bridges at night without any arms is out of the question as far as our men are concerned, they are nevertheless anxious and willing to be of practical use to the military authorities. The same spirit which animated them when we offered to guard the bridges originally still prevails and whatever duties they are called on by the Garrison Commander will be done willingly and effectively. I am much obliged for your kind references to the way our men discharged their duty from which we are now relieved and would ask you when communicating with General Hill to kindly convey to him our thanks for his courtesy.

58 De Róiste, Liam, 'Mar Is Cuimin Liom', part 32, in *The Evening Echo*, 4 December 1954.
59 Florence O'Donoghue's biography of Tomás MacCurtain lists the following as the first brigade officers, 'Tomás MacCurtain, Commandant; Daithí Barry, Adjutant; and Seán Murphy, Quartermaster.' On the publication of that book this information was refuted by The Cork 1916 Men's Association. On page three of their 'Comments on Florence O'Donoghue's life of Tomás MacCurtain' they list the first brigade officers as, 'Tomás MacCurtain, Terence MacSwiney, Seán O'Sullivan, Seán Murphy, Seán Jennings and Pat Ahern. MacSwiney's position as second-in-command to MacCurtain is also recorded on page 34 of his biography written by Moirin Chavasse. Liam de Róiste on the other hand in 'Mar Is Cuimin Liom', part 33 in the *Evening Echo*, 9 December 1954 names Seán O'Sullivan as vice-commandant. It is our view that the organisation of the Brigade Staff cited in this text represents the correct version.
60 Liam de Róiste Diary, Cork Archives Institute, ref: U271/A/16.
61 O'Donoghue, Florence, *Tomás MacCurtain*, p. 60.
62 De Róiste, Liam, 'Mar Is Cuimin Liom', part 33, in *The Evening Echo*, 9 December 1954.
63 Ibid., part 34, in *The Evening Echo*, 11 December 1954.
64 Ibid.
65 *The Cork Examiner*, 27 March 1915.
66 De Róiste, Liam, 'Mar Is Cuimin Liom', part 34, in *The Evening Echo*, 11 December 1954.
67 The Cork City Battalion was augmented by sections of Volunteers from the rural companies.
68 De Róiste, Liam, 'Mar Is Cuimin Liom', part 34.
69 In his diary entry for 4 June 1915, Liam de Róiste notes his opinion that Fawsitt was sent to America by, 'the anti-Volunteer element of the IDA'.
70 De Róiste, Liam, 'Mar Is Cuimin Liom', part 34.
71 *Cork Examiner*, 24 May 1915.
72 Ibid.
73 De Róiste, Liam, 'Mar Is Cuimin Liom', part 34.
74 Liam de Róiste Diary, Cork Archives Institute, ref: U271/A/17. De Róiste's diary entry for 13 June also reveals the state of the relationship that existed between Fawsitt and MacSwiney at that time. 'MacS is till very sore regarding F. They did not agree when F. was at home and F's going to America has incensed MacS.'
75 O'Donoghue, Florence, *Tomás MacCurtain*, p. 61.
76 Ibid., p. 62.
77 Born in Rosscarbery, Co. Cork in 1831, O'Donovan Rossa worked distributing relief during the Great Famine of 1845–49. In 1853 he founded the Phoenix National and Literary Societies which were later assimilated into the IRB in 1858. He became a leading organiser with the organisation and was imprisoned from 1865–71 during which time he was elected to parliament for Co. Tipperary (1869). Upon his release he went to America where he organised a 'skirmishing fund' to

finance a Fenian bombing campaign in England (1881–85). He launched vitriolic attacks on British rule in Ireland trough the pages of *United Ireland* and travelled America lecturing on this subject. He visited Ireland in 1894 and in 1904 but returned to New York where he died on 30 June 1915.

78 Edwards, Ruth Dudley, *Patrick Pearse – The Triumph of Failure*, (Poolbeg Press, Dublin 1977) p. 237.
79 De Róiste, Liam, 'Mar Is Cuimin Liom', part 38, in *The Evening Echo*, 30 December 1954.
80 Chavasse, Moirin, *Terence MacSwiney*, p. 34.
81 O'Hegarty, P. S. *A Short Memoir of Terence MacSwiney*, The Talbot Press, Dublin 1922, p. 59.
82 Liam de Róiste Diary, Cork Archives Institute, ref: U271/A/17.
83 Ruiseal, Liam, *The Position in Cork*, p. 374.
84 Liam de Róiste Diary, Cork Archives Institute, ref: U271/A/17.
85 *Ibid.*
86 Chavasse, Moirin, *Terence MacSwiney*, p. 35.
87 Meaney, Cornelius, Witness Statement No. 64 Bureau of Military History.
88 *Ibid.*
89 Ruiseal, Liam, *The Position in Cork*, pp. 374–5.
90 *Ibid.*
91 *Cork Examiner*, 29 November 1915.
92 Cork City, Glanworth, Macroom, Courtbrack, Ballinadee, Mallow, Lyre, Ballinhassig, Kanturk, Donoughmore, Cobh, Tracton, Crookstown, Tullylease, Fermoy, Kilmona, Clogough, and Mourne Abbey.
93 Born in Scregg, Kiltyclogher, Co. Leitrim in 1884, MacDermott was inducted into the IRB by Bulmer Hobson in 1906 and became a full time organiser of that organisation in 1908. He was joint founder and editor of *Irish Freedom* in 1910 and although an attack of polio left him disabled in 1912 he was closely involved in the formation of the Irish Volunteers a year later. Before addressing the Manchester Martyr meeting in Cork he had served four months hard labour having been arrested in Tuam on 18 May 1915 for making an 'anti-recruiting' speech.
94 *Cork Examiner*, 29 November 1915.

5 – Rebellion

1 Chavasse, Moirin, *Terence MacSwiney*, p. 37.
2 *The Irish Volunteer*, 8 January 1916 – copy in Cork Public Museum ref: no. 1966.64.
3 On p. 69 of his biography of MacCurtain, O'Donoghue states 'It is not clear under what auspices the lecture was held but Tadgh Barry was actively associated with the arrangements, and Seán O'Sullivan, the city battalion commandant, appears to have approved of it. As neither MacCurtain nor MacSwiney attended, the lecture does not appear to have been given official brigade sanction'.
4 Subsequently referred to after the Easter Rising as 'The Military Council'.
5 O'Donoghue, Florence, *Tomás MacCurtain*, p. 73.
6 *Cork Constitution*, 15 March 1916.
7 *Ibid.*
8 *Cork Examiner*, 16 March 1916.
9 Original document in Cork Public Museum ref: 1666.3422.
10 *Cork Examiner*, 16 March 1916.
11 Cork City, Mitchelstown, Mourneabbey, Glenville, Dunmanway, Lyre, Clogagh, Bandon, Kilpatrick, Ballinaspittle, Millstreet, Ballinhassig, Macroom, Dooisky, Carrigannima, Clondrohid, Ballingeary, Courtbrack, Garryvoe, Donoughmore, Ballynoe, Dungourney, Clonmult and Midleton.
12 O'Donoghue, Florence; *Tomás MacCurtain*, p. 70; 'The Irish Volunteers in Cork 1913–1916', in *The Journal of the Cork Historical and Archaeological Society*, Vol. IXXI, p. 42.
13 'The Irish Volunteers in Cork 1913–1916', p. 42.
14 O'Donoghue, Florence, *Tomás MacCurtain*, pp. 77–78.
15 *Ibid.*, p. 78–79.
16 *Ibid.*, p. 79.
17 *Ibid.*, p. 84.
18 *Sunday Independent*, 23 April 1916.
19 Seamus Fitzgerald papers, Cork Archives Institute, ref: PR/6/40.
20 *Ibid.*, ref: PR/6/45 (5).
21 Langford Papers, Cork Archives Institute, ref: U 156.
22 O'Donoghue, Florence, *Tomás MacCurtain*, p. 95.

23 *Ibid.*, p. 98.

24 Feeney, P. J., *Glory O, Glory O, Ye Bold Fenian Men*, p. 48.

25 *Account of Easter Week 1916* compiled by Seán Murphy on behalf of Cork 1916 Men's Association, 3 November 1956.

26 Transcript of diary kept by Tomás MacCurtain, Cork Public Museum, ref: no. L. 1945.226.

27 *Ibid.*

28 Langford Papers, Cork Archives Institute, ref: no. U 156.

29 Wash, J. J., *Recollections*, pp. 37–38.

30 *Transcript of MacCurtain Diary*, Cork Public Museum, ref: no. L. 1945.229.

31 *Account of Easter Week 1916* compiled by Seán Murphy.

32 Letter from Bishop Coholan in the *Cork Free Press*, 20 May 1916.

33 Transcript of MacCurtain Diary, Cork Public Museum, ref: no. L. 1945.229.

34 Letter from Bishop Coholan in the *Cork Free Press*, 20 May 1916.

35 Chavasse, Moirin, *Terence MacSwiney*, p. 63.

36 Letter from Bishop in the *Cork Free Press*, 20 May 1916. On page 114 of his biography of MacCurtain, O'Donoghue states that the last condition was secured by Butterfield and Coholan on their own initiative and without the knowledge of the Volunteer leaders.

37 *Cork Constitution*, 29 April 1916.

38 Letter from Bishop Coholan in the *Cork Free Press*, 20 May 1916.

39 *Ibid.*

40 *Ibid.*

41 Langford Papers, Cork Archives Institute, ref: no. U 156.

42 *Account of Easter Week 1916* compiled by Seán Murphy states that, 'Nearing the end of that week when the negotiations initiated by the Bishop and the Lord Mayor with the British military authorities had been agreed upon, an order was issued by the local Brigade Council to the Cork Volunteers that no magazine rifles or ammunition was to be handed over to the Lord Mayor. This order was strictly adhered to.'

6 – Aftermath

1 Cornelius Collins, Daithí Cotter, Donal Óg O'Callaghan, Christopher O'Gorman, Seán Nolan, Fred Murray, Cornelius Murphy, James Murphy and Patrick Trahey. Mary MacSwiney, the president of Cumann na mBan and Nora O'Brien, the secretary were also arrested in Cork that Tuesday.

2 *Cork Free Press*, 20 May 1916.

3 Pádraig and Jack Hyde from Ballinhassig, Co. Cork.

4 See O'Donoghue, Florence; *Tomás MacCurtain*, pp. 119–120 and Chavasse, Moirin; *Terence MacSwiney*, pp. 77, 78.

5 Seamus Fitzgerald papers, Cork Archives Institute, ref: no. PR/6/45 (5).

6 *Ibid.*

7 Transcript of Tomás MacCurtain Diary, Cork Public Museum, ref: no. L. 1945.P.29.

8 *Ibid*

9 *Ibid.*

10 The last executions, those of James Connolly and Seán MacDermott took place on 12 May 1916.

11 Appendix B lists the Volunteer prisoners from Cork, the date of their arrival in Britain and the prison in which they were initially incarcerated.

12 *Ibid.*